A High Tech Business Venture: Startup, Growth and Closure

A High Tech Business Venture: Startup, Growth and Closure

My Preparation for the Business Venture

Haripada Dhar

Copyright © 2018 by Haripada Dhar.

ISBN: Softcover   978-1-9845-1769-2
           eBook   978-1-9845-1768-5

All rights reserved. No part of this book may be reproduced or transmitted in any form or by any means, electronic or mechanical, including photocopying, recording, or by any information storage and retrieval system, without permission in writing from the copyright owner.

This is a work of fiction. Names, characters, places and incidents either are the product of the author's imagination or are used fictitiously, and any resemblance to any actual persons, living or dead, events, or locales is entirely coincidental.

Any people depicted in stock imagery provided by Getty Images are models, and such images are being used for illustrative purposes only. Certain stock imagery © Getty Images.

Print information available on the last page.

Rev. date: 08/05/2020

To order additional copies of this book, contact:
Xlibris
1-888-795-4274
www.Xlibris.com
Orders@Xlibris.com
776867

Contents

Preface ix

My Preparation for the Business Venture 1
Growth of Urgency for the Business Venture 4
The Business Venture 8
Competitive Submission 13
Non-Disclosure and Warranty Agreement 19
Gradual Achievements in Offering Products 22
Business Plan 27
Fuel Cell Operation: 3W-5V System (model FCS104) 55
Operation of 300W Forced-Flow Fuel Cell Stack (model FCS6420) 60
Fuel Cell Operation: 1kW stack (model: 250-24) 68
Health Issues 79
New Business Location and Business Closure 81

Biography of Haripada Dhar 83
References 89

Dedication

My business venture history may be of particular interests to entrepreneurs in the high technology areas. As a case history of business conception, development and closure, it may of interest to many. Each business has its unique characteristics. All businesses together make up the economy of the country, just as little drops of water make the mighty ocean. I dedicate this book to all.

Haripada Dhar
October 2017

Preface

From conception of a novel idea to the production and marketing of kilowatt range fuel cells (PEM or proton exchange membrane) and related products were achieved in the business venture. The urge of starting a business came from the momentum generated through suffering of being laid off in a job and going through the changes from job to job for a few years. Finding an innovative idea for the business, establishing the business, get funding for the development of the business, making and selling products—these are all steps of entrepreneurship. Some people may be an entrepreneur naturally, others may learn from the family tradition, and still others may get it from the inner urgings. Establishing a business in the high technology area, in particular, starting it from the scratch requires proper education, training, strong motivation and personal drive. It requires a tremendous push from various sources to start a business. If one does not have that urge, entrepreneurship may not be possible for him/her.

Another important motivation for having my own business was to give my family a stable environment for living. I suffered a lot during the period I was looking for a job and was moving from one place to another. I moved from Toronto (Canada) to Texas (USA); Texas to Connecticut, from there to Arizona, and then to California, and back to Texas. Such moving around (and the instability it creates) is not favorable for the dependents and, in particular, children in their formative ages. If they do not have to move, they would be more secure and stable. It took about 15 years after my Ph.D. education when I was able to start my own business. Coming from a third world country was another disadvantage for me for many things I did or could not do.

It was worthwhile for me to make an attempt to write this book on starting a high tech business and continuing it for some time. The attempt required indomitable determination, adequate training, personal sufferings, rejection from employers, and experiences of poverty and discrimination. I consider myself fortunate and well-rewarded to be able to establish myself as a leader in the fuel cell industry, the chosen area of my expertise.

A business plan, an important part of a high tech business for attracting capital investment is also included in the write-up.

In the innovative concept, the sales of fuel cells depended very much on the ease of operation of fuel cells. Self-humidification is one aspect, which made fuel cell operation easier and simplified the control of other variables. Operational guide of three classes of fuel cells from 3W to 1kW have been included as a way of demonstrating achievements in the business growth.

A competitive submission for a recognition award brings out the subtle and important points on the basic innovation concept of the business venture. Even though the submission did not result in an award, the attempt illustrates the novelty of the venture.

The fuel cell industry, in general, did not see an exciting growth; many were expecting to see in the nineties and early twenties perhaps due to the lack of acceptance of the product lines using hydrogen, which is known to be explosive in nature. The acceptance of fuel cells may grow at a slower pace, and ultimately catch up when effects of depletion of fossil fuels are intensely felt.

Certain health problems of mine overtook me, and I ended up having a heart double-bypass surgery in early 2010. The surgery may not have gone well with me; I did not fully recuperate timely. The scar tissues (keloids) limited my movements and activities. At the end of 2011, the business venture closed after about 22 years of operation.

My Preparation for the Business Venture

Starting a business or the task of entrepreneurship requires the urge of motivation gained by going through some personal suffering. In the high technology area of a business it requires appropriate education and sufficient experience gathered from employment in one or more businesses. If that is all needed for an incentive for starting a business, then it is all right and acceptable. In my case, it was not easy to put myself in a position that would help me to start a high tech business venture. Let me explain.

I was born and brought up in a third world Asian country (Bangladesh) where poverty was rampant. We were fortunate to have a high school in our area. I received free tuition, and my education was facilitated. My elder brother (Nimai Chand Dhar) joined my father's efforts of supporting the family. Without my elder brother's sacrifice I could not have finished my high school education even with free tuition. In the school final examination, I got scholarship which supported my education at Ananda Mohan College, Bangladesh. After two years of college final, I got another scholarship that supported my education at Dhaka University and my expenses at the Jagannath Hall university residence. After my Master's degree, I got a job as a researcher at the Council of Scientific and Industrial Research (CSIR). There I met Dr. Arun Kumar Basak, who was an employee with the CSIR at the supervisory level. Dr. Basak received M. S. degree from St. Francis Xavier University and Ph.D. from University of New Brunswick. Both universities are located in Canada.

According to the recommendation of Dr. Basak, I wrote to Dr. E. A. Secco at the St. Francis Xavier University, Antigonish, Nova Scotia,

Canada. I got accepted by Dr. Secco in the Master's program. I did not have to send applications in many places. I got admission in 1967 and graduated in 1969.

Dr. Basak lent me about half of the air fare for my travel from Dhaka to Halifax. I also received financial help to defray my air fare from another person in Dhaka. He was a businessman. He encouraged me and he was glad that I was admitted for higher education abroad. It is worth mentioning his contribution to my career. In those days, he offered me "cornflakes and milk" as a treat for snacks. At that time, it was the first time in my life I had this kind of a treat. I received encouragement from another businessman to go ahead for higher education abroad. I paid off all my financial debts gradually from income of my studentship. It is to be mentioned here that later when I was able to establish a business and was in a stable financial condition, I extended invitation to Dr. Basak to visit my Company recognizing his contributions to my career. He was perhaps having health problems; did not respond to my invitation. I was willing to pay for all his expenses including that of accommodation for a month.

It was the first flight experience for me – my journey to Halifax from Dhaka. Making an international flight to a western country was another step forward. From Dhaka I flew to Karachi, Pakistan, and stayed overnight in a hotel. My next flight took me to London and stayed in a hotel. My flight from London to Halifax was not confirmed which I did not know until I arrived in London. I got a last minute seat on the plane. From Halifax airport, I had to take a taxi to the train station in Halifax. The taxi trip took most of my twenty dollars; I was allowed to carry with me. The train took me to Antigonish, my destination, around midnight. After this long travel, I was kind of sick. The university authority put me to the infirmary for a few days. My parents and the family were in agony for two to three weeks until they received my first letter.

After the Master's program, I got admitted to the Ph.D. program at the University of Ottawa under the mentorship of Dr. Brian E. Conway, who was an Electrochemist. I worked in his laboratory in the area of electrical double layer studies. At the end of 1973, I got my Ph.D. degree. During the studentship at the University of Ottawa, my family was displaced from the troubled country, East Pakistan to India as a result of the civil war for the liberation of Bangladesh from Pakistan. After my Ph.D. program,

I went to see my displaced family in India. They got relatively stabilized. I got married in 1974. I tried for a job in Canada without any success. Dr. Conway indicated that a university teaching job would not be suitable for me.

I was offered a post-doctoral fellowship with Dr. Alan Bewick at the University of Southampton, in England. At the end of two years (1975-1976) of fellowship, I tried to obtain a regular employment with a corporation and government research laboratories in Canada without any success. Dr. Secco knowing my condition that I did not get any job offered me a temporary fellowship, so that I could come back to Canada with an employment. He was kind. My electrochemical background at that time became a mismatch at the Dr. Secco's laboratory. I desperately I tried to find an employment with a corporation. I got a job with a company, HSA Reactors Ltd. in Toronto. I worked there for two years. Because of the company's insufficient funding situation, I was told to look for a job. I decided to try for a job in the United States. Dr. John O'M. Bockris was at the Chemistry Department of Texas A&M University. I wrote him, and he offered me a research position. Towards the end of 1979, I came to the United States. Dr. Bockris helped me with my immigration (Green Card), and later with my US Citizenship. At Texas A&M University, I also worked with Dr. Ronald Darby and Dr. Ralph White, both of the Chemical Engineering Department. I have a patent on the prevention of electrochemical prevention of bacterial-fouling and a few publications with Dr. Bockris. I have publications also with Dr. Darby and Dr. White.

Growth of Urgency for the Business Venture

My search for a corporate position in the USA became successful when I obtained a job as a Research Scientist with Energy Research Corporation (ERC) in Danbury, Connecticut. My job was to do research work in the fundamentals of fuel cell reactions involving hydrogen and air (oxygen). Fuel cells are energy devices for clean, non-toxic, alternative energy. I made five publications, presented papers in meetings. However, I was unable to secure a good relationship with my immediate supervisor, whose qualifications were less than that of mine. When a downturn came for the company, I was called in to a meeting with the Vice President and was informed that I had to leave—I have been laid off from the job. It was a shock and disappointment. At that time, I worked at ERC for four years, 1984-1987. During this period, I purchased a house (condominium) and I had a family: my wife and two children. Despite showing the best in the company, bad news came to me. I did not expect what did happen to me and my position with the company. However, importantly I got the determination to have my own business sometime. But it was not easy.

Years later, when I was able to establish my own business in a high technology area, ERC was impressed. ERC personnel communicated with me often and purchased our fuel cell products. I was on the point of being invited by ERC for a visit. However, that did not happen.

I started looking for a job. I wish I did not have to move. If the family did not have to move, they would feel more stable and secure. I received a call from Los Angeles. The person was associated with a small company in Yuma, Arizona. Rather quickly, he wanted me to go there and join the company, and paid for the fare. Soon, I made a long trip from New York to Los Angeles, and went to their office in the LA area. I waited a few hours in their office. In a private air plane we flew from LA airport to Yuma at 10-11 PM. After this lengthy and tiring travel, Danbury to Yuma, I was taken to a hotel for the night. The following day I joined the company. I worked there for a few months. The company was a startup one, was not having sufficient funds and was unstable. The company was lacking sufficient ideas for a new technology for attracting funding from government or private sources. It did not suit me there.

A small business in Los Angeles hired me following a telephone interview. From Yuma I moved to LA. After a few months, when I was preparing to move my family to LA, I received a call and later a job offer from Dr. John Appleby of Texas A&M University (TAMU). He was the Director of the Center for Electrochemical Systems and Hydrogen Research (CESHR) and Professor of Applied Electrochemistry at TAMU. He was also the President of a company, Ementeck, Inc. having the core business in the development of batteries. A part of the Dr. Appleby's letter (dated August 20, 1987) I quote below:

"It is with great pleasure that I make an offer of appointment to you as Senior Scientist for Ementeck. The salary for this position is $35,000 per annum. In addition, you are entitled to a fringe benefit program up to 24% of your salary, and you will benefit from a share in any invention disclosures that you might produce, to be negotiated. We all sincerely hope you decide to accept this offer, Hari. We are extremely anxious to have you with us and move rapidly ahead with implementation of our company. Your technical expertise will be a vital part of this development."

I accepted the offer of Dr. Appleby. I moved to College Station, Texas to join Ementeck, Inc. My family moved from Danbury to College Station. It was our second coming to College Station after an absence of about five years. While I was at Ementeck or a few years earlier, Dr. Oliver Murphy along with Dr. Duncan Hitchens established a company called Lynntech. Both of them were with Dr. Bockris as Post-Doctoral Associates. Lynntech eventually succeeded to be well established a medium size company obtaining many awards from government agencies.

With my contributions for further progress of Ementeck, the Board of Directors of the company were planning to expand the company getting more funding from individual donors and becoming a public company in the future. The officials seemed to have ignored me hiring another individual over me. I decided, it was not possible to continue with Ementeck, and submitted my resignation (dated September 28, 1989). A part of the letter I quote here: "I have been with Ementeck for two years from the beginning of operation of this company. To work for a startup business was not an easy job, particularly, when the laboratory was empty. I hope my hard work for the company was an important factor that contributed to the additional financing, the company is about to receive. I also felt that recent changes in the company have stunted hopes of my further growth which was the prime objective of my accepting your job offer with a new company."

Being in the Bryan-College Station area, I was in the middle of start-up companies: Ementeck, Lynntech. There was a business incubator in the area. I got the courage to start my own business. I along with three other partners, I established a company named Biotech Resources, Inc. on April 19, 1988; and won an SBIR (small business innovative research) Phase I award. My limited background in the biotechnology did not allow me to continue in that direction. Having accumulated some cash from the operation of Biotech Resources, I cofounded along with Dr. D. H. Lewis of Veterinary Microbiology Department, Texas A&M University on October 6, 1989 a company named BCS Technology, Inc. The landmark event in my life occurred about 15 years after my Ph.D. education. I rented some space in the Business Incubator of the Bryan-College Station area. I talked to the Director of the NASA funded Center for Space Power of the Texas A&M University for some funding for the development of the innovative concept I had. Based on a proposal for work on the development of self-humidified proton exchange membrane (PEM) fuel cells, I was approved for a NASA-funded small grant. Dr. Bockris who was also a member of the Board of Directors of Ementeck, sent me a congratulatory note (dated October 8, 1990), which I quote: "I am very glad to hear that you have got a grant. Now you have got to make it a great success and go ahead and get lots more."

The beginning of BCS Technology was the start of my corporate life. With the motto of starting small and thinking big I continued business for 22 years. After about two years of the startup, Dr. Lewis, who was a professor at Texas A&M, resigned due to the mismatch of our backgrounds. After about 10 years of the startup, the company was named BCS Fuel

Cells, Inc. since the prominent business was in the area of simplified fuel cell products. Developing, making and selling products, having patents on inventions, applying for and securing grants allowed maintaining the business.

I attained a status in the ladder of learning in the western world that attracted along with many, the attention of my mentor, Dr. Bockris, who wrote me a letter (dated May 26, 2009). I quote a part of this letter here: "Of the many electrochemists I have known, you have been out of perhaps three who have really shown that you could make it, i.e., that you could come out into the struggle which is public life in the USA and come out on top".

The CSP of Texas A&M helped the startup of my business. The Research Foundation of the university came up levying royalty charges on the company. Royalties to be paid on the sales of products incorporating the patent rights in whole or in part would be 1%. The royalty rate would increase to 5% if the company is able to license the technology to any third party.

The Business Venture

The Opportunity

The core technology of the Company was based on operations of PEM (proton exchange membrane) fuel cells, in particular, fuel cell operations without requiring humidification. The invention offered a great opportunity for investment, marketing, and further development of the technology.

The Technology

The Company developed the technique of self-humidified operation of PEM fuel cells, and the technology of building and operating fuel cell stacks. Normally, the PEM fuel cell is operated with humidification. Extra pure water is supplied to the fuel cell. The process requires an auxiliary system, which adds to the fuel cell weight and volume. In the BCS-developed method, the membrane-electrode assembly in the fuel cell absorbs a portion of the water produced in the fuel cell. This absorbed water assists in the self-humidified operation. Fuel cells can be operated up to 70ºC instead of 80ºC when the fuel cell was operated under humidified conditions. The Company also developed its own method for preparation of electrodes and membrane-electrode assemblies (MEAs) for making the fuel cell stack.

In a convection fuel cell stack, the attractive feature offered was the elimination of an air compressor (pump), which creates power draw on the fuel cell and reduces its overall efficiency.

BCS Products could be operated under dead-ended conditions of hydrogen with periodic release. Hydrogen does not flow out of the stack during the short dead-end period. During the much shorter release period, hydrogen, water vapor, and other diluent gases are released. This process increases the utilization of hydrogen to about 98-99%.

Competitive Position

The Company enjoyed the competitive advantage in the type of PEM fuel cells and components it offered. These were self-humidified type fuel cells, and membrane-electrode assemblies. The competitors, even though, were able to offer larger fuel cell stacks, needed to humidify the stacks. The Company needed to offer larger and compact stacks, and needed to offer a complete power source utilizing a fuel cell stack.

The Market

The PEM fuel cells will have appeal to users for various purposes. Some of these applications will be in the following areas: (1) portable power sources in the range of 10W to 1kW for recreational uses, for variable sign messages for the transportation sectors, and back pack power for the military and space applications. (2) Standby power sources in the range 2kW-10kW for residential applications. (3) Mobile power sources in the range of 50kW-80kW for electrical vehicles. The market for fuel cells is small compared to the total usage of all forms of energy. The demands for fuel cell based power units expected to increase, particularly, for the simplified type, which will be easier to operate. The concept of distributed generation is becoming popular among the utility companies. The fuel cell stands to benefit tremendously supplying power sources as the medium of distributed power. The residential market is ready, subject to some regulatory scrutiny from the state and local government. Each of the above main three areas represents a large market in the $10's of millions.

As of this writing (year 2017), the fuel cell market did not grow much for the last 10 years. As a consequence, the shares of companies those went public are trading at the lower range of the yearly fluctuations. In future, the fuel cell market sure to improve as the fossil fuels deplete.

Employees at the Early Stage of Business

At the early stage of Company operations, there were three employees who shared the management responsibility of the Company. Hari Dhar was the president of the Company. With a Ph.D. in Electrochemistry, as the inventor of the technology, Dhar possessed the skills and vision to work effectively in the emerging fuel cell market. Dhar was aided in the research and marketing of products by Siva Chokkaram, who had a Ph.D. in Chemistry with a background in catalysis. He had been working with the Company building and operating stacks. Ms. Krishna Dhar was excellent in making electrodes and MEAs. She also helped in assembling fuel cell stacks. As the company operation grows, the Company needs to hire more personnel for R&D, manufacturing and sales. A CPA firm maintained Company accounting. The Company also worked with a firm having expertise in electronics and building control units.

Fuel Cell Products Offered

BCS Fuel Cells offered the following Products:

- Convection (air breathing) fuel cell stacks
- Regular forced-flow fuel cell stacks
- Forced-flow stacks operating with H_2/O_2
- Control boxes for stacks
- Membrane-electrode assemblies (5-layer and 3-layer kinds)
- Electrolyzers
- Reversible fuel cell stacks
- Test Bench/Demonstrator unit

Marketing Plan

The Company initially marketed small fuel cell stacks and membrane-electrode assemblies. Customers included a few companies making their own products, such as such as sensors and small fuel cell stacks using BCS-supplied MEAs. This is the initial stage of marketing, thus building customer relationships and customer-confidence in BCS products. The order of entry into the market would be offering of smaller stacks, and then larger ones. In this way the Company would gain experience in the marketing of its fuel cell products. The Company would be well positioned to enter into the market of offering standby power sources for residential applications. The Company advertised in the Internet maintaining a web site, and also in trade journals, and preparing brochures, distributed in fuel cell meetings. The interactions and responses received from customers were encouraging in that the customers liked BCS stacks and MEAs.

A List of Available Fuel Cells with Model Numbers

The fuel cell details including peak power (W) and voltage (V) information are given in two tables below. Performance and stability data of each stack were obtained and provided to customers.

Convection type stacks						
Stack	Model #	Area(cm^2)	Current (A)	Volt (V)	Power (W)	Peak W,V
4-cell	10-4	10	2	2.5	5	8, 2.4
10-cell	10-10	10	2	6.0	12	15, 6
20-cell	10-20	10	2.5	12	30	35, 12
4-cell	25-4	25	4.5	2.6	12	15, 2.4
10-cell	25-10	25	5	6.5	30	36, 6
20-cell	25-20	25	4.6	13	60	70, 12
10-cell	50-10	50	9	6.5	60	70, 6
18-cell	50-18	50	8	12.5	100	120, 12
24-cell	50-24	50	10	15	150	170, 13

Forced-flow type stacks						
Stack	Model #	Area (cm²)	Current (A)	Volt (V)	Power (W)	Peak W,V
10-cell	64-10	64	25	6.5	150	160, 6
20-cell	64-20	64	25	12.5	300	320, 12
32-cell	64-32	64	25	20	500	600, 18
34-cell H_2/O_2	64-34	64	35	24	800	880, 22
24-cell	250-24	250	65	16	1000	1400, 15

Visitors Who Came to Our Lab

Many visitors from various places came to see our operations of building fuel cells.

- Snead Research Institute, Austin, Texas.
- Hydra Fuel Cells, Oregon.
- NASA, Houston, Texas.
- Texas A&M University, College Station, Texas.
- University of Texas, Austin, Texas.
- Japan
- South Korea
- Spain
- England
- Saudi Arabia
- India
- Ford Motor Company
- Avista laboratories, Spokane, Washington
- Plug Power and Ballard Technology – visited us at the early stage of the company.
- One elderly couple vacationing in Texas came to see our business for generating clean energy using fuel cells. Our Company operation was worth seeing for them.

Competitive Submission

The following was submitted to a company in the USA for consideration of a recognition award:

1. Name of Submission
"Self-Humidified PEM Fuel Cells"

2. Function and Distinctive Benefits

PEM fuel cells, both convection (also known as air breathing) and forced-flow types can be operated without requiring additional humidification of the reactants, air and hydrogen. As is well-known, ordinarily, PEM fuel cells would require external water for humidification of reactants for their operation. This humidification step can be avoided using the developed technology.

The distinctive benefits are as follows:

- Fuel cell operation becomes comparatively easier and uncomplicated: make the fuel cell, pass the reactants, and activate the fuel cell instantaneously for power output.
- Fuel cell becomes more efficient as it saves the consumption of the extra power needed for the external humidification in regular fuel cells.
- The process leads to no consumption of additional water during fuel cell operation. Water generated internally by

the fuel cell reaction is utilized in a self-humidified fuel cell.
- A fuel cell system with the complete balance of plant becomes compact, lightweight, and of lower cost.

3. Patents

Four US patents were granted on self-humidification and related studies. Patent number with their expiration dates are given below:

- 5,242.764 (2011)
- 5,381,863 (2012)
- 5,521,030 (2014)
- 5,935,725 (2017)

4. How widespread are Commercial Applications? What to Expect in the Future?

BCS Fuel Cells, Inc. makes sales of its smaller fuel cells up to about 500W to educational institutions and corporations. The educational institutions purchase mainly to teach their students operation of fuel cells easier way (self-humidified). Students do some projects for their degree. Corporations may use these fuel cells for specific applications; for example, evaluate the success of their own projects on hydrogen generation from hydrocarbon sources or from water.

The future of self-humidified fuel cells is expected to be brighter and more extensive than the regular humidified kinds, particularly, for applications requiring quick power output. Such an application may include the mini-missile technology of the military. BCS is a participant supplying self-humidified MEAs for such an application. At the present, markets of all fuel cells are developing. The market for self-humidified fuel cells is also developing keeping in pace with the overall market.

5. Strength of Submission, and Degree of Innovation

A significant innovation was achieved over a number of years. The innovation is based on Nafion products, which are used in our MEAs. Such MEAs have been given the terminology self-humidified

MEAs. We operated fuel cells self-humidified at a time when very few people tried to operate or thought it was possible. At the present time, many use thin membrane (0.001 inch thick) to operate under self-humidified conditions, but are usually limited to maximum of about 50°C. Our operation goes from ambient to about 70°C using a thicker membrane, Nafion 212 (0.002 inch). The initial demonstration of self-humidification was with a hole in a membrane and through deposition of Nafion solution around the hole. The cell worked self-humidified. Gradually, membranes of various thicknesses without holes were used making improved deposition of catalyst on the micro-porous layer of the GDL. The cell temperatures of our initial fuel cells were low, about 40°C. Our present self-humidified fuel cells perform much improved and operate up to about 70°C. We won SBIR Phase I and Phase II grants from the NSF for the work on self-humidification. We won a 4-year term grant from the DOE along with a group of other companies. Our task was to improve the operation of our self-humidified fuel cells.

A few relevant references are given below:

1. H. P. Dhar. "On solid polymer fuel cells." J. Electroanal. Chem., 357(1993)237-250.
2. H. P. Dhar. "Medium term stability testing of PEM fuel cell stacks as independent power units." J. Power Sources, 143(2005)185-190. Please see also references therein.
3. H. P. Dhar and S. K. Chaudhuri. "Detections of electrode flooding in single cell experiments through measurements of cell internal resistances." Extended Abstract for Poster Presentation, Fuel Cell Seminar (2008), Phoenix, AZ

Two plots demonstrating operation of self-humidified fuel cells are given below:

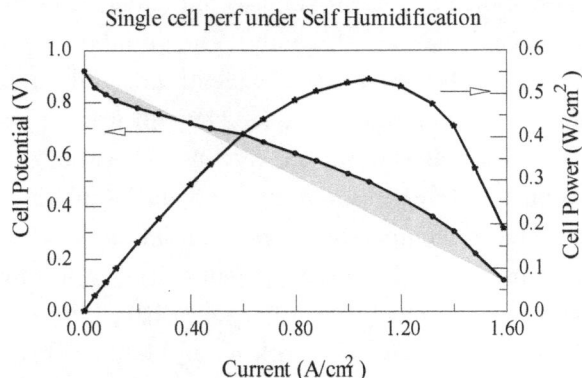

Electrode active area: 25 cm^2
Air stoich: 1.75
Air P: 8 psig
Hydrogen P: 3 psig
T: 60° C
Anode: 0.2 mg/cm^2, Cathode: 0.5 mg/cm^2 Pt

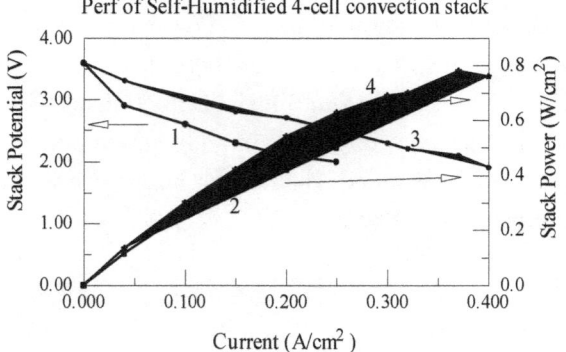

Electrode active area: 10 cm^2
Air flow by convection
Hydrogen P: 2 psig
Hydrogen dead-ended (30 sec) with periodic release
T: Lines 1 & 2, 42° C
  Lines 3 & 4, 65° C

6. Strong Points of the Submission

Particularly that electrodes can be made using a machine, self-humidified fuel cells will have the same commercial potential as the regular standard fuel cells requiring external humidification.

Self-humidified fuel cells would be sustainable by their own advantages mentioned earlier. The electrodes for the self-humidified fuel cells can be made on larger scale using a machine, such as the one BCS had from Coatema Corporation of Germany. It was a lab-scale machine and could coat catalysts on GDL of sizes 38 cm x 22 cm on a platen size of 40 cm x 24 cm. The proprietary process of coating could be extended to larger sizes with a bigger machine. We developed the process of making rapid electrodes with various catalyst loadings using the lab-scale machine. BCS not only used self-humidified MEAs for its needs, but also sold in quantities of 10-50 to a customer. Thus the process of making self-humidified MEAs has been made quicker at lower costs and a number of customer bases have grown, making the self-humidified fuel cells a sustainable product.

The technology can be applied for making MEAs not only for self-humidified fuel cells, but also for MEAs for fuel cell operation utilizing humidification.

7. Strength of Submission With Respect to Breadth of Use

Self-humidified fuel cells will satisfy a niche market where a quick power output is required without the complications of supplying humidification. Presently, the temperature range is 70°C. At present, smaller fuel cells are offered for sale up to about 1kW or are being evaluated in a research project. After the success of smaller fuel cells, larger fuel cells would be tested and offered for sale. There is no inherent limit to the application for self-humidified fuel cells. However, it would be most suitable for applications needing immediate power output under simplified operating conditions possibly utilizing power within about 250W. BCS was involved in a project supplying MEAs to a customer working on mini-missile technology for the military. The power sources would be suitable for uses by the military in unmanned underwater vehicles and remotely operated vehicles for airborne and submarine deployed applications. Power units could also be used as backpack power for the military and space explorations. The general public will find numerous applications as a portable power source, for example, portable electronics, computer power, power for recreational uses, and electrical equipment.

Non-Disclosure and Warranty Agreement

A typical agreement between the Company and a customer who would purchase BCS products:

The Customer wants to purchase one fuel cell stack (warranty agreement applies to certain models) from the Seller. Terms and conditions for the purchase are as follows:

1. Seller BCS Fuel Cells, Inc. warrants that the fuel cell, its components, and technology contained therein (herein referred to as "Fuel Cell") purchased and delivered shall be free from defects for a period of 6 months from the date of delivery to the Customer subject to Section 2 of this Agreement. During the warranty period, Seller shall repair any defects to the Fuel Cell unless such defect solely was caused by Customer.
2. Customer must take adequate precaution during its use. The following items shall not be subjected to the warranty even if they are caused within the warranty period: 1. Failure caused by a natural disaster, accident, collision, normal wear, fuel contamination, air contamination, transportation accident, or deterioration; 2. Normal deterioration in the cell performance that can occur with time; 3. Failure caused by incorrect handling during operation, misuse, neglect, alteration, dismantling or modification; 4. Improper storage, abnormal conditions of operations; 5. Failure to conform to the operation and maintenance manual.

3. Customer assumes all risks and liability for loss, damages, or injury to persons or to property of the Customer or others arising out of the use or presence of the fuel cell purchased hereunder.
4. Customer agrees not to remove BCS labels from the fuel cell stack and other products.
5. Customer agrees that the Fuel Cell is proprietary of the Seller and shall use reasonable care to hold in confidence and not disclose the Fuel Cell unless permitted by Seller. CUSTOMER acknowledges that the technology, and all information relating to the business and operations of the BCS fuel cells that CUSTOMER learns or has learned during or prior to the term of this Agreement, may be the valuable, confidential, and proprietary information of the BCS. Customer's obligations set forth herein shall extend for ten (10) years from the initial date of disclosure hereunder and shall be considered satisfied if Customer uses the same degree of care to protect and avoid disclosure of similar proprietary information as Customer uses to protect and avoid disclosure of its own proprietary information.
6. This agreement by CUSTOMER applies to CUSTOMER's successors, collaborators, customers, employees, and agents, who may be using the fuel cell stack.
7. Seller agrees that Customer shall have no obligation of confidentiality with respect to Fuel Cell if: (a) such information is a part of the public domain without a breach of this Agreement by Customer; or (b) such information in known to Customer at the time Seller discloses it to Customer; or (c) such information is independently developed by Customer; or (d) such information is received by Customer from a third party who had a lawful right to disclose such information to Customer; or (e) such information is disclosed by Seller to any third party, including the United States Government, without restriction as to further disclosure; or (f) such information is disclosed to a third party with the written approval of Seller.
8. Neither party shall be liable to the other for the disclosure of Fuel Cell that is obligated to be disclosed by order of a court of competent jurisdiction.

9. This Agreement will be governed by and construed in accordance with Texas, USA law, without regard to the principles of conflict of laws.
10. This Agreement and the attached purchase order contain the entire understanding between the parties, and supersede any prior agreements, oral or written. This Agreement may not be modified, except by written amendment duly executed by an authorized representative of each party.

Gradual Achievements in Offering Products

The Company was in the business of developing, designing, testing, and fabricating PEM fuel cells. The Company developed and produced reliable fuel cells, as well as and MEAs (membrane-electrode assemblies), and PEM-based MEAs for direct methanol fuel cells (DMFCs), electrolyzers, and reversible fuel cells.

Depending upon user preference and end use, the choice of an MEA for a particular application could be of the three-layer type, known as catalyst coated membrane (CCM), or the five-layer type.

BCS Fuel Cells specialized in self-humidified-operation of fuel cells; however, the company's products included MEAs for both standard and self-humidified operations. Conventional PEM fuel cells require continuous water input in the form of water vapor during operation. Self-humidified technology allows fuel cell systems to operate more simply and efficiently than that of a fuel cell requiring outside humidification, enabling, for instance, remote installation. For example, simply by adding a control unit for regulation of hydrogen flow to a company's convection fuel cell stack, it can be turned into a self-starting power generator requiring only a supply of hydrogen. The self-humidification technology is based on a unique, patented MEA-type developed by the company, as well as other design features.

The Company offered smaller fuel cells stacks and systems and high-performing membrane-electrode assemblies for various applications, the major types of which have been mentioned earlier above. A fuel cell stack can be a regular-forced flow type (requiring forced-flows of hydrogen and air) or a convection-type (requiring air flow by convection/forced convection, and forced flow of hydrogen). PEM fuel cells offered by the company could be operated up to about 70ºC under self-humidified conditions.

Applications of both convection and forced-flow fuel cells include, but are not limited to, academic research, educational and public demonstrations of clean energy, portable power generator, uninterrupted power supplies, backup and regular power generators.

The Company has been granted four patents on its technologies of self-humidification, membrane-electrode assembly, electrode preparation, and convection stack assembly.

Products

Three-layer electrolyzer MEA

In general, in production of the three-layer type MEA, catalysts are pressed on both sides of the membrane. Such an MEA is commonly known as catalyst-coated membrane (CCM). During assembly of the cell stack, appropriate contacts need to be placed on each side of the CCM. If the contact is a gas diffusion layer, it can, in some cases, pressed onto the CCM prior to stack assembly, creating better contacts with the catalyst layers.

A CCM can be used for

(a) PEM fuel cell
(b) Electrolyzer
(c) Reversible PEM fuel cell (can be operated as a PEM fuel cell and also as an electrolyzer)
(d) DMFC

For a CCM to be used in an electrolyzer, the catalyst on one side would be Pt, and on the opposite side, IrOx. On the Pt side, hydrogen is evolved, and on the IrOx side oxygen is evolved. The Pt side behaves as a cathode (negative electrode), and the IrOx side behaves as an anode (positive electrode).

Three-layer reversible CCM for PEM fuel cell and electrolyzer

A reversible PEM fuel cell can be used as an electrolyzer and also as a PEM fuel cell. The cell/stack design has to be correct so that a proper contact is made when operated as an electrolyzer and also when operated as a fuel cell. The catalyst on the hydrogen side is Pt and on oxygen side, the catalyst is a proprietary mixture of Pt and IrOx. When operated as an electrolyzer, the cell polarity is as mentioned above. When operated as a fuel cell, the Pt catalyst side is the fuel cell anode (negative electrode) where hydrogen is consumed, and the opposite side is the fuel cell cathode (positive electrode) where oxygen is consumed.

Three-layer and Five-layer MEA for DMFC (direct methanol fuel cell)

Membrane-electrode assemblies for the DMFC were offered in the three-layer and five-layer forms, based on customer preference and end use. On the anode side (negative electrode), the catalyst was Pt/Ru; on the cathode side (positive electrode), the catalyst was Pt.

Three-layer and five-layer MEA for standard PEM Fuel Cells

To operate a fuel cell with a standard-type MEA, both sides of the MEA would require humidification. Such an MEA was offered in the three- and 5-layer forms.

Five-layer MEA for a self-humidified PEM Fuel Cells

To operate a fuel cell with a self-humidified-type MEA, the fuel cell could be operated without humidification. Operational conditions must be carefully controlled for such operation: temperature up to 70°C, lower air stoichiometry, hydrogen dead-ended with periodic release and a certain pressure on both air and hydrogen sides.

Fuel cell systems

Two kinds of fuel cell stacks or systems were offered. A fuel cell stack could be a convection type or a forced-flow type. In the convection type, only hydrogen flow is forced; air is passed into the fuel cell by convection/forced-convection. In the forced-flow type, both reactants: air and hydrogen, were forced into the fuel cell.

Fuel cell system (convection type)

A fuel cell system could be made very simple, using just a convection fuel cell stack. A control unit for regulating hydrogen dead-ended with periodic release could be incorporated with the fuel cell to make the assembly a convection-type fuel cell system. The fuel cell system becomes an independent power unit and can be started by just passing hydrogen into the fuel cell. The needs for start-up power and for the subsequent stack-cooling are supplied by the fuel cell through the control unit.

Fuel cell system (forced-flow type)

A hydrogen control unit could be incorporated with a forced-flow type fuel cell stack to regulate the hydrogen flow dead-ended with periodic release. The control unit could be powered from the fuel cell stack. The stack, however, does not become an independent power unit, as required power for cooling and air passage is not provided by the simple control unit mentioned here.

Control units for fuel cell stacks

A control unit, powered by the fuel cell stack, was used to regulate the flow of hydrogen and to power the cooling fans. The power unit comprised a pressure regulator, which maintained a set pressure inside the stack. In addition, it had two functions: driving the cooling fans for the convection stacks and regulating the purging cycle for hydrogen in the dead-ended mode of operation of the fuel cell. The dead-end time can be varied from 4 sec to 40 sec.

A control unit could be used for both convection and forced-flow stacks.

Fuel Cell Test Bench/Demonstrator (Model TB1100)

The Company offered a Test Bench for evaluating fuel cells. It was a one switch startup and one-knob control Test Bench for fuel cells up to capacity of about 2kW. It offered a choice of AC power line 120V/60 Hz or 230V/50 Hz. It was a low cost alternative to expensive stations, yet offered fairly advanced monitoring functions, such as air and hydrogen flow, stack temperature, voltage and current. Flow pressure regulators, analog output cable for computer connections, a cooling unit, air filter, air compressor, connecting tubes, and electrical connections were the standard items supplied with Test Bench. Automatic stack cooling at preset temperatures could be conducted.

Business Plan

1. Executive Summary

BCS Fuel Cells, Inc. (the Company or BCS) was a privately owned small business, incorporated in the State of Texas. BCS was established from the scratch to conduct development work on PEM (proton exchange membrane) fuel cells. The Company developed technologies to produce various kinds of membrane-electrode assemblies (MEAs). Such MEAs have a number of applications: PEM fuel cells, electrolyzers, direct methanol fuel cells (DMFCs), and reversible fuel cells. A break-through product was the self-humidified PEM fuel cell, which is much simpler to operate. The simplification is achieved through self-humidification, which eliminates water management in the fuel cell, and brings in desirable features of easier operation, maintenance, and cost reduction. The SWOTT (strength, weakness, opportunity, threat, and trend) analysis indicated that the Company had strengths in a number of areas and had taken a lead in offering reliable self-humidified fuel cell products and components, primarily, high performing MEAs. The Company would participate in a large market, which was expected to grow. There are four patents on the technology of self-humidification, membrane-electrode assembly, electrode preparation, and convection stack assembly.

Within the month of August 2009, the Company relocated locally to a larger facility in one acre land, completely owned by the Company. This presented opportunity for growth in the technology and production areas in the future.

The Company mission was to become a leader in the PEM fuel cell industry offering simplified, better performing, and more economical products. The Company wanted to capture a major market share, and thereby bring about a change in the fuel cell market dominated by the present players.

The products to be offered by the Company included the following:

- Fuel cell components, such as electrodes and MEAs.
- PEM fuel cell stacks and systems.

The PEM fuel cell is a clean energy-producing device, using hydrogen as the fuel. The fuel hydrogen is abundantly available from water, natural gas, propane, gasoline, etc.

The power sources offered by BCS would be of the simplified type requiring only minimum of water management. The cost would be lower than that of the competition because of simplification. The FAB (feature, advantage, and benefit) analysis indicated favorable characteristics of BCS fuel cells: lower cost, easier repair, more power output, and selection preferences by the customer.

The Company had been offering smaller fuel cell stacks of capacities 3W to 1000W for some time. The Company would like to enlarge its business of making MEAs and improve the feature of self-humidification of its fuel cells, and fuel cell systems for various applications. The demands for distributed power generation will grow. The fuel cell market is expected to reach $25 billion/year by 2025 in U.S. alone. BCS expected to capture 1-2% on the initial market, increasing market share significantly with time.

The Company was seeking capital of $3 million for mass production of its MEA series.

1.1 Objectives

One of the objectives of the Company was to become a leading supplier of 5-layer MEAs for building self-humidified PEM fuel cells. Additional objectives were to be able to supply 3-layer MEAs for PEM fuel cells, for electrolyzers, and reversible fuel cells. Objectives also included becoming a leading supplier of simplified portable fuel cells, and achieving sales of $1M from various products in the next 5 year.

1.2 Technology

In the fuel cell industry, the Company offered products based on a unique technology of self-humidification or decreased humidification. Based on this technology, the products can be of the following types:

- Membrane Electrode Assemblies (MEAs), and
- Fuel cell stacks.

Membrane Electrode Assemblies

The Company developed a number of processes for making MEAs that could be used for making self-humidified PEM fuel cells.

An MEA could be of the following two broad categories:

- The traditional 5-layer type MEA. It consisted of two catalyst-coated gas diffusion layers hot-pressed against a centrally placed membrane.
- The 3-layer type MEA. It consisted of two coatings of catalysts facing each other directly on a membrane. It is also known as catalyst coated membrane (or CCM).

In the 5-layer type, BCS offered MEAs of the following categories:

- Standard 5-layer MEA suitable for use in PEM fuel cells requiring humidification.
- Self-humidified 5-layer MEA suitable for use in PEM fuel cells requiring no humidification.
- The 5-layer MEA suitable for use in direct methanol fuel cell (DMFC) applications.

In the 3-layer type, BCS offered MEAs of the following categories:

- The 3-layer MEA suitable for applications in self-humidified and humidified PEM fuel cells.
- The 3-layer MEA suitable for applications in electrolyzers.
- The 3-layer MEA suitable for applications in reversible fuel cells.

Fuel Cell Stacks

Under the fuel cell stack category, BCS offered two classes of fuel cell stacks as follows:

- Convection stacks. The stack required only the flow of hydrogen, it picked up air from the atmosphere.
- Forced-flow stacks. This class of stacks operated under forced-flow of both air and hydrogen.

In the fuel cell stack category, the fuel cell could be Convection type and Forced-flow type.

1. Convection type fuel cells: 3W to 150W. Such a fuel cell required the input of only hydrogen; it picked up air from the atmosphere. These fuel cells could be used for various portable applications.
2. Conventional forced-flow type fuel cells: 150W to 1kW or larger. Such a fuel cell required the input of both reactants hydrogen and air. Such fuel cells could be used for portable, residential, industrial, and mobile applications.

The user of a fuel cell had the flexibility of installing the power supply at his/her location, and use it as the demand for power arises. When there was a low demand of power, fuel cell operated at a high efficiency 60-70%. With demand increasing, the efficiency may drop to 50-55% range, which was still higher than other energy sources.

The efficiency of recovering both electricity and heat was over 90%. The lifetime of these fuel cells is expected to be the same as other PEM fuel cells: about 5-10 years or longer. The BCS-offered fuel cells were characterized by simplicity of operations having no need for a continuous feed of water humidification in them. In regular PEM fuel cells, a continuous feed of pure water is maintained to keep them humidified. This is the so-called water management process, inherent in a PEM fuel cell stack. The self-humidification developed by BCS eliminated the humidification step, and thus simplified the fuel cell operation and its maintenance. The water management in BCS-produced fuel cells was simplified: it consisted only of the removal of product water. The consumer would greatly benefit from any simplification in the design, operation, or maintenance of a power source. Thus consumer preferences for simplified products will lead to greater sales and profits.

The Company also operated fuel cell stacks with synthetic reformates (equivalent to fuel compositions from natural gas or propane), and found that PEM fuel cells can be operated under self-humidified conditions with such dilute fuels. Self-humidified operation can be extended to thin and thick membranes.

1.3 Competitive Advantages

The competitive advantages of self-humidification were the following:

- Startup, operation, and maintenance of a fuel cell became easier due to the absence of water management.
- Stacks had lower volume and weight by up to 20%.
- System cost was lower because of simplification.
- There would be an overall higher power output because of less parasitic loss.
- Fewer components lead to greater reliability.

1.4 Certain Limitations of the Technology

There are certain limitations to self-humidification at the present stage of development as follows:

- Temperature limit to 70°C vs. 80°C for the humidified PEM fuel cells.

- Operation at the lower stoichiometry of air is required to conserve the water in the fuel cell.

These limitations, however, could be brought to favorable conditions. For example, providing humidification at a much reduced rate to the fuel cell could increase the operating temperature to 80°C. The fuel cell operation at a lower stoichiometry of air could be considered a desirable feature because such operation would conserve the parasitic power needed for the high flow of air into the fuel cell stack.

1.5 Market/Marketing

The fuel cell industry offers a large market covering applications in the portable, stationary, and mobile applications. Virtually, any application of power is a potential market. Since the possibilities are so great, the Company initially focused on producing portable power systems up to 1kW of net power, and on supplying various MEAs to other producers of fuel cells and electrolyzers.

It was estimated that about 1 to 1.5 billion people worldwide have no access to the grid power. Most grid systems in developing countries cannot cope up with the demands resulting in frequent power blackouts. The high cost of extending the power grid limits the rate of electrification.

Assuming about 1% of 1 billion people willing and able to buy a fuel cell power and that on the average of 10 people per family, a million households are potential customers. Add to this the millions of small shops, farms, and offices in the world, and the markets for small power systems can easily reach the multi-billion-dollar range.

The potential uses of PEM stacks can be classified in three categories. (1) Portable power sources will be used for recreational uses, variable message signs in the transportation sector, backpacks for the military and space flights, electronic applications, etc. (2) PEM stacks as power sources will supply power to homes and industries, and as (3) mobile power sources to electrical vehicles.

The Company was targeting the portable power sources market requiring power up to 1kW capacities. At the same time, BCS emphasized the marketing of its various MEA products. The improved categories of various MEAs mentioned above can both supply internal use and external sales to other fuel cell companies.

The fuel cell-based power sources appeal to the users as the clean power source. Initial demands were expected to come from hobbyists, fuel cell enthusiasts, pioneers, environmentalists, corporations, schools, colleges, universities, and wealthy individuals.

1.6 Sources/Uses of Funds and Exit strategy

The Company was seeking an initial investment of $3 million. The Company had been basically an R&D company, taking time to develop the technology and its products. Now, the technology being ready, the priorities needed to be adjusted to become primarily a manufacturing company to offer products at much lower costs.

With the available funds, the Company would

- Purchase equipment to mass-produce electrodes and MEAs.
- Produce complete fuel cell systems.
- Increase technical, sales, and marketing staff.
- The exit strategies for investors include the following:
- Merger with or acquisition by another company.
- Possible IPO (initial public offering) offering.

2. Company and Technology

The Company activities and its technology upon which the activities were based on have been discussed below in the following subsections.

1.1 Brief Company Introduction

BCS Fuel Cells, Inc. (referred to as BCS or the Company) was a privately owned small business, incorporated in the state of Texas. The Company started operation as BCS Technology 1989 engaging wholly in the development of PEM (proton exchange membrane) fuel cells. BCS was also involved in production and marketing of PEM fuel cells and its major components, membrane-electrode assemblies (MEAs). The PEM fuel cell is a clean and efficient energy producing device operating in the temperature range of 0-80°C. This range is most convenient for many practical applications of a power source. The fuel cell has all solid components, and is a rugged device. The Company produces power sources from simplified fuel cell stacks, which are easier to operate and maintain, compared to the standard PEM fuel cells. The proprietary stack is self-humidified, requiring only minimum of water management, and is therefore lightweight and has a lower cost compared to the standard PEM type.

A PEM fuel cell would normally require continuous humidification from an external source for its operation. It becomes an involved operation and increases the system volume and weight. Besides, there is the likelihood of the fuel cell contamination from the continuous input of external water source into the fuel cell. A self-humidified fuel cell, on the other hand, does not need any external humidification, and its operation becomes considerably simplified.

The fuel cell uses hydrogen as the fuel and air as the oxidant. Byproducts are water and heat. Hydrogen is abundantly available from water, methanol, natural gas, propane, gasoline, etc.

2.2 Company History

The Company activities started through the accumulated sweat equity of Dr. Haripada Dhar, the cofounder of the Company. The Company received a grant from the NASA-funded Center for Space Power (CSP), Texas A&M University, for simplifying PEM fuel cells through self-humidification. The CSP has awarded several small grants for the development of PEM fuel cells and stacks. The company received several SBIR grants, which helped to make progress in the vital R&D work leading to a stage of offering fuel cell stacks and components for sale.

The Company collaborated with Texas A&M University, sold many small stacks and membrane-membrane electrode assemblies to many customers, thus validating the approach of self-humidification. BCS was a subcontractor of two research grants received by the Center for Electrochemical Systems and Hydrogen Research (CESHR), Texas

A&M University, for optimization of fuel cells and membrane-electrode assemblies. CESHR was also subcontractor of a grant received by BCS.

2.3 Analysis of Strength and Weakness

The SWOTT (strength, weakness, opportunities, threats, and trends) analysis indicated that the Company has strength in a number of areas and took a lead in offering reliable fuel cell products. BCS needed to offer products, which could make a complete a power source, ready to be used with appropriate fuel cell reactants. The Company would participate in a large market. The possible threats are from companies developing self-humidification in fuel cells, and from companies developing high efficiency combustion engines. The latter is a general threat to the fuel cell market.

The Company was ahead of its competitors in the self-humidified technology by at least five years of development work. The company was continually improving its self-humidification technology increasing the versatility of operation, for example, temperature and pressure ranges of stack operation. The Company could produce both self-humidified type and standard type MEAs, mentioned earlier.

The self-humidification technology had the following advantages:

- Easier stack operation due to absence of water management required for the fuel cells that need humidification of reactants.
- Lower stack volume and weight by about 25%.
- Higher overall power output because of less parasitic loss of power. It is estimated that at least 10-15% more power output could be achieved because of the savings from the parasitic loss.
- Better quality of the produced water because of absence of its dilution by any incoming water.

At present, the Company offerings included fuel cell stacks with power conditioning. The company will make partnerships with companies producing fuel processors.

2.4 Fuel Cell Technology Overview

In principle, a fuel cell operates like a battery. Unlike a battery, a fuel cell does not run down or require charging. It will produce energy in the form of electricity and heat as long as fuel, hydrogen, and another reactant, oxygen or air, are passed into the fuel cell.

A PEM fuel cell consists of two electrodes, anode and cathode, sandwiched around a membrane electrolyte. Oxygen passes over the anode and hydrogen over the cathode, generating electricity. Water and heat are the byproducts. The anode and cathode contains appropriate catalysts for the fuel cell reaction to occur.

$$H_2 = 2\,H^+ + 2\,e$$
$$2\,H^+ + 2\,e + \tfrac{1}{2}\,O_2 = H_2O + \text{electricity} + \text{heat}$$

Electrodes are of the gas diffusion type containing the catalyst and are bonded to both sides of the membrane thus producing the membrane-electrode assembly (MEA). Alternatively, catalysts are applied directly on the membrane producing a catalyst coated membrane (CCM).

A single cell is completed by current collector plates, which contain machined flow fields, as required for effective distribution for reactant gases along the surface of the electrodes. The current collector plates become bipolar plates in a fuel cell stack, in which case they would have gas flow fields on both sides.

2.5 Types of Fuel Cells

There are several basic types of fuel cells. These include:

Phosphoric Acid. This type of fuel cell uses phosphoric acid as the electrolyte. The operating temperature is up to 200°C.

Proton Exchange Membrane. (PEM). This type of fuel cell uses a proton conducting membrane as the electrolyte and operates at relatively low temperatures up to about 80°C. PEM fuel cells can vary the output quickly to meet shifts in power demand, and are suited for applications, -- such as in automobiles -- where quick startup is required.

Molten Carbonate. Molten carbonate fuel cells promise high fuel-to-electricity efficiencies and operate at about 650°C. Such fuel cells have the capability of using hydrocarbon fuels directly without going through the reforming process and are suitable for multi-MW applications.

Solid Oxide. Another highly promising fuel cell, the solid oxide fuel cell (SOFC) could be used in big, high-power applications including industrial and large-scale central electricity generating stations. SOF works at temperatures up to 1000°C.

Alkaline. Long used by NASA on space missions, these cells can achieve power generating efficiencies of up to 70 percent. They use alkaline potassium hydroxide as the electrolyte. This kind of fuel cells is susceptible to poisoning by carbon dioxide gas.

Direct Methanol Fuel Cells. These cells are similar to the PEM cells in that they both use a polymer membrane as the electrolyte. However, in the DMFC, the anode catalyst itself draws the hydrogen from the liquid methanol, eliminating the need for a fuel reformer. Efficiencies of about 40% are expected with this type of fuel cell, which would typically operate at a The temperature range for this fuel cell is 40 to 65°C.

Regenerative Fuel Cells. Still a very young member of the fuel cell family, regenerative fuel cells would be attractive as a closed-loop form of power generation. Water is separated into hydrogen and oxygen by a solar-powered electrolyzer. The hydrogen and oxygen are fed into the fuel cell which generates electricity, heat and water. The water is then recirculated back to the solar-powered electrolyzer and the process begins again.

2.6 Patents

The Company was granted four U.S. patents on its technology of self-humidification, membrane-electrode assembly, electrode preparation, and convection stack assembly. The granted patents are the following:

1. Near ambient, unhumidified solid polymer fuel cell. H. P. Dhar. U.S. Patent No 5,242,764 (1993)
2. Near ambient, unhumidified solid polymer fuel cell. H. P. Dhar. U.S. Patent No. 5,318,863 (1994).

3. A method for catalyzing a gas diffusion electrode. H. P. Dhar. U.S. Patent No 5,521,020 (1996).
4. Flow facilitator for improving operation of a fuel cell. H. P. Dhar and K. A. Lewinski. U.S. Patent No. 5,935,725 (1999).

3. Commercialization Strategy

The commercialization strategy has been discussed in the following sections below:

3.1 Factors Affecting Commercialization

The key factors affecting fuel cell commercialization are cost, reliability, and availability of fuel, hydrogen.

The cost of the BCS-produced fuel cell stack and the system would be lower because of the elimination of the external humidification of the fuel cell. Lower cost would make fuel cells more attractive for mission critical applications like standby power for communications and put fuel cell prices within the reach of average consumers and small businesses. Other commercial applications of fuel cells included portable power sources, powering portable electronics and other electronic equipment, computer power, and fuel cell demonstrations. Lower price and improved performance of Company's products would give a strong competitive edge in the market.

For the supply of hydrogen fuel, reforming of hydrocarbons, like natural gas, propane, etc. was an option. The reformed fuel thus produced contains a mixture of hydrogen, CO_2, and nitrogen. Hydrogen generators using cheap power, like solar or hydro were another option of getting pure hydrogen for fuel cell applications.

3.2 Product Development

The Company purchased raw materials such as gas diffusion layers and membranes from suppliers and made its needed supply of MEAs for sales and for making fuel cells.

There were numerous companies interested in purchasing MEAs from suppliers. These companies did not have the MEA technology of their own, or needed a better product, so were dependent on outside suppliers. Therefore, the various types of MEAs offered by BCS Fuel Cells could form a major part of its business income. However, the technology must be extended to larger scale production.

The company had a lab scale coating machine for producing electrodes. Of immediate importance was the rapid production of electrodes and MEAs by Company proprietary methods. As the demand for MEAs and fuel cells increased, a large number of MEAs needed to be produced rapidly. To achieve this objective, the Company needed to introduce automation in producing electrodes and assembling membrane-electrode assemblies. For this purpose, equipment suitable for continuous coating and laminating needed to be purchased.

3.3 Packaging of Products

The Company recognized that attractive packaging was an important part of the marketing strategy. The system packaging would be tailored to the particular targeted market. Residential units would be housed in a durable and attractive housing that would look nice if mounted outside a home. Industrial designers would be used early in the design process to create attractively styled housings that each contained essentially the same components.

Industrial units would contain the same components as a residential unit in a rugged skid mounted housing that allows the addition of more stacks to expand the power supply. The skid base allowed the unit to be mounted in the same manner as typical machine tools and allowed multiple units to be linked together. This feature would keep the cost of expansion low and encourage customer loyalty.

3.4 Strategy for Bringing Down Price Acceptable to End Users

The commercialization of fuel cells would depend on the affordable and competitive pricing of the fuel cell system. Presently, the pricing was higher than that of the conventional energy sources, primarily because of the cost of raw materials, and of low volume production. These costs would decrease dramatically on high volume production. Also, the simplified nature of the system would contribute to cost reduction. Additional factors for cost reduction were to increase the performance of the fuel cell stack, and increase the efficiency of power conversion, proper utilization of byproducts heat and water.

4. Customers

Fuel cells could be built in various sizes: 1W to several hundred kilowatts. Thus, fuel cells would have appeal to users of various categories.

- In the lower end of the range, fuel cell would serve as an alternative power supplies to batteries. Direct methanol fuel cells were already being used to replace cell-phone batteries.
- Fuel cells in the range to 3W-500W would fulfill the needs for uses as portable power sources for applications, such as, backpack power for the military and space explorations, power for recreational uses and electrical equipment.
- Fuel cells in the range of 500W to 3kW would be used for supplying needs for smaller industries, meeting certain needs of electrical vehicles, and as uninterrupted power supplies (UPS) for under water applications.
- Power units in the range of 3kW-10kW would be used as decentralized power sources to residential customers.
- The power units in the range 50kW-80kW would be used to build engines for electrical vehicles.
- Units in the range of 200kW-1000kW or higher would be used as power station for providing power to a community, village, shopping center, hospital, apartment buildings, etc.

The customer base of the Company would be both domestic and international.

A few small businesses were customers of the Company purchasing self-humidified MEAs. These companies were Ardica Technologies, TDM, and Clean Fuel Cell Energy. Fuel Cell Store, a distributor of Company's products was also a major buyer of MEA products.

5. The Market and Marketing Strategy

5.1 Market Analysis

The fuel cell industry is relatively new, and comes under the general area of power sources. As mentioned earlier, there are several types of fuel cells: phosphoric acid, molten carbonate, PEM, alkaline, and solid oxide. These classes of fuel cells are at the various stages of development. The phosphoric acid and alkaline are possibly the most developed. The other three types can be considered moving parallel to commercialization stages. The PEM is the most versatile kind being capable of manufactured into different power capacities: fraction of a watt to megawatt ranges.

The market for fuel cells is theoretically unlimited. Any device that requires power could use a fuel cell. Realistically, since fuel cells are not the best for most economical choice for every application, the current market is much more limited. The most suitable applications for fuel cells at this time are remote locations, grid supplementation (peak shaving) and standby or backup power. As the cost of fuel cells come down the market will widen.

The competitors to fuel cells are solar and wind power. Life of these systems is expected to be the same as the life of a fuel cell, estimated to be about 10 years. The Company's price/kW and operational costs will be made competitive with solar and wind power with the added advantages of waste heat, indifference to weather and an at-hand gas supply.

The waste heat from fuel cells will be of great use for residential applications providing home heating and hot water requirements. Placement of fuel cells in major industrial plants, crowded cities or locations should reduce loading on the electrical grid, and at the same time provide more dependable power sources. The fuel cell industry should receive favorable incentives from EPA (Environmental Protection Agency), DOE (Department of Energy), PUC (Public Utility Commission) and the State NRCC (Natural Resources Conservation Commission).

A number of publications are appearing with discussions on the development of the fuel cell industry. A few of these publications are *Fuel Cells Bulletin* (Elsevier Science), *Fuel Cell Industry Report* (Scientific American), *Fuel Cell Technology News* (Business Communications Co.), *NFCRC Journal* (National Fuel Cell Research Center, University of California, Irvine), Bulletins published by Fuel Cells 2000 group, and publications by US Fuel Cell Council.

The current market for fuel cells is small compared to the total usage of all forms of energy. The projected sale of fuel cells in various categories expected to reach $25 billion/year by 2025 in the US alone.

5.2 Market Segmentation

To establish its position in the market, the Company would initially select a target geographical region of the US that met the criteria of the marketing strategy. The team would focus on specific target groups within this region. The target selection criteria were:

- Affluent, educated populace.
- Environmentally aware populace.
- Regional need to conserve water.
- Rapid regional growth, preferably with a large percentage of rural/semi-rural developments.
- Readily available gas supply.
- High electric rates or rates for installation of service.
- States supporting net-metering or offering attractive alternative energy incentives.

The fuel cell market would eventually transcend geographical boundaries, and would extend to all countries of the world. In countries outside North America, fuel cells of sizes 3kW-4kW can be used to provide power to homes, as there would be less demand for power utilization. BCS established contacts in many countries for distributing BCS fuel cell units.

5.3 Market Strategy

The potential uses of PEM stacks could be classified in three categories. (1) Portable power sources will be used for recreational uses, variable message signs in the transportation sector, backpacks for the military and space flights, electronic applications, etc. (2) PEM stacks as power sources will supply power to homes and industries, and as (3) mobile power sources to electrical vehicles.

The Company was targeting the portable power sources market requiring power up to 1kW capacities. At the same time, BCS would emphasize the marketing of its various MEA products.

The products would be marketed through the BCS Fuel Cells, Inc. web site, advertisement in professional magazines, and through brochures, distributors, presentations, and word-of-mouth. BCS worked with five distributors: one in the Unites States, one in Japan, one in Korea, one in Singapore, and one in Taiwan.

The fuel cell-based power sources appeal to the users as the clean power source. Initial demands would come from hobbyists, fuel cell enthusiasts, pioneers, environmentalists, corporations, schools, colleges, universities, and wealthy individuals.

There is a surge of public interest in fuel cells and clean energies, and in particular, hybrid power involving fuel cells and batteries. BCS received many inquiries for use of fuel cells in supplying power to homes, in particular, new homes, vacation homes and those in remote locations. Thus, the distributed generation of power, free from the utility grid, is becoming a popular concept. The deregulation of the power industry would provide an impetus to the distributed power generation, and the fuel cell would immensely benefit becoming a medium of distributed power.

There is a certain amount of phobia from the general population for using hydrogen as an energy source. The public will get assured of the safety of fuel cells using possibly small portable fuel cells. This would be followed by use of medium size fuel cells in the range 3-10kW units for residential applications. The applications of fuel cell in automobiles will follow. However, BCS would be ready to enter into any market opportunities that may develop, which was not anticipated.

The Company would perform most business functions: contract R&D, manufacturing, and sales. The control of the Company will be shared with equity investors.

The Company would be in need of capitals. The Company would be open to all possible financing methods such as given below:

1. Technology licensing.
2. Strategic alliances.
3. Equity investment in the Company by interested parties – sweat equity.
4. Private placement of stock.

5.4 Product Differentiation

The power sources offered by BCS would be of the simplified types requiring only minimum of water management. Because of simplification, the cost will be lower compared to that of the competition. The stacks would have control systems, which will allow near 99% utilization of the fuel hydrogen. The active electrode area of a cell would be such that when a stack is assembled, it generates a sufficient voltage at full power of the stack, so that in many cases power conversion may not be necessary. For example, one 3kW stack will operate at 30V at full power output. This stack will not need a voltage converter, and will be able to operate with standard components of rating 24V.

5.5 Why People Would Buy BCS Products

BCS offered simplified fuel cell stacks. People would prefer simplified products, which are easier to operate and maintain. Additional incentives are environmental concerns, high efficiency, tax credits or incentives, pure water, expandability, reduced reliance on the electrical power grid, and reduced cost to many users.

6. Competitors

The competitors for fuel cells are the other power generators: batteries, generators based on the limitation of Carnot's cycles. The generators based on the heat-engines are limited by Carnot's cycles and have lower efficiencies than that of fuel cells. The fuel cells enjoy high efficiency of conversions, and are therefore favorable as the power source.

The following are the competitors in this country (USA) in the area of PEM fuel cells:

1. Ballard power – portable, residential, and mobile, and larger power sources
2. Plug Power – residential, and mobile power sources
3. Ion Power – catalyst coated membranes
4. Electrochem – smaller power sources, test stations
5. Reli-on Power – residential power sources
6. W. L. Gore Associates – membrane, catalyst coated membranes

The Company enjoyed the competitive advantage in the type of PEM fuel cells and components it offered for sale. BCS was one of the few PEM fuel cell companies offering products for sale. The competition, even though, is able to offer larger stacks, need to humidify them. Self-humidified fuel cells offered by a few companies, for example, operate up to a lower temperature limit of 45-50°C (opposed to 70°C for BCS products). The lower temperature operation requires more cooling of the fuel cell to remove the generated heat. Thus the fuel cell uses a greater power to run its accessories, in the process decreasing the actual power output of the stack. Thus the usefulness of low-temperature self-humidified fuel cells is limited. BCS needs to offer larger and more compact stacks.

The FAB (Features, Advantages, and Benefits) analysis given below indicated favorable characteristics of the Company's MEAs and fuel cells.

FAB Analysis of Company's MEAs

Item/product	Feature	Advantage	Benefit
5-layer MEA	Self-humidification	Water management simplified	Easy operation
	High performance	Reliable stack assembly	Lower cost
	Requiring humidification	Offers choices to customers	Flexibility in product development
MEA for DMFC	High performance	Require less number of MEAs for a particular power output	Lower cost
3-layer MEA	For PEM fuel cells	Provides alternate supplies from BCS	Source of more revenue to BCS, lower cost to customers
	For electrolyzers	Provides alternate supplies from BCS	Source of more revenue to BCS, lower cost to customers
	For reversible fuel cells	Provides alternate supplies from BCS	Source of more revenue to BCS, lower cost to customers

FAB Analysis of Company's Fuel Cells

Item	Feature	Advantage	Benefit
Fuel cells	self-humidification	Water management simplified	Easy operation
	MEA technology	MEA fabrication with variable catalyst loading	(a) lower cost (b) easier repair

| | high performance | Low voltage loss with dilute reactants | More power output |
| | thin and thick membranes | Offer choices of electrolytes | Customer has selection preferences |

The following table compares a few features of the Company's fuel cells with that of the competition.

Feature	The Company	Competition
Water management	1. Self-humidified 2. Water removal only	1. Humidification required 2. Water addition and removal
MEA	Owns MEA technology	Dependent on suppliers

7. Marketing and Sales Plan

The immediate marketing and sales objectives were the following:

1. Sale of various types of MEAs the Company produces.
2. Sales of portable fuel cell stacks (convection type): capacity 3W–150W.
3. Sales of portable fuel cell stacks (regular forced-flow type): capacity 100W-1000W.

7.1 Intensive Selling Efforts

Intensive selling efforts would be made through the following:

1. Advertisement

BCS maintained a web site in the Internet, advertised in the trade journals, and attended meetings. BCS would make an intensive advertisement effort as larger fuel cell stacks were built.

2. Product brochures

Attractive product brochures would be made featuring stacks of various sizes.

3. Direct mailing

As part of the advertisement efforts, product brochures would be mailed to selected customers in industries.

4. Emphasize feature, advantage, and benefit of BCS products
5. Sales and marketing team

BCS would need a sale and marketing team for distribution of its products. BCS provided six months of warranty on all products. In future, the warranty would be raised to one year or more.

BCS would need sales representatives in the future.

7.2 Pricing

Pricing is crucial to gain entry into the market. With production facilities in countries with cheaper labor, it would be possible to reduce prices to become affordable to the general population. With the simplified fuel cell stack using its in-house MEAs produced in larger quantities, and mass production fuel cells, the Company would have price advantages over the competition.

The fuel cells were at the initial stage of commercialization. The prices were considered high at that stage. The reasons are that the raw materials were expensive, and volume of production was low. Individual units were built as orders were received from customers. With the volume increasing, the price would come down drastically.

8. R&D Plan

The objectives were to continue development efforts of membrane-electrode assemblies and PEM fuel cells. Some of these efforts were to achieve better self-humidification, high performance, better reactant flows, lightweight stack components, effective stack cooling, turn-key operation, system development, etc. Also, mass production of components, such as membrane-electrode assemblies (MEAs) and separator (bipolar) plates would be required for cost reduction.

8.1 Better Self-Humidification

The goal would be to increase the temperature range for self-humidification, so that less cooling of the fuel cell stack was required. Better membranes capable of operating at a higher temperature than that presently available would be required. Many institutions are presently involved in the development of membranes. Also, a better stack design may contribute to better self-humidification.

8.2 Higher Performance of Fuel Cells

Higher performance would depend on better catalysts and their distribution on electrodes. BCS would be ready to take advantage of the availability of better catalysts and distribution techniques on electrodes.

8.3 Better Reactant Flows

This would depend on the design of a better flow patterns for the fuel cell reactants. The pressure-drops across the fuel cell stack should be minimal, so that the reactant gases can flow easily through the stack without expending much energy from the fuel cell stack.

8.4 Lightweight Stack Components

The fuel cell stack needs to be made lightweight, sturdy, and compact. The primary raw material at this time is graphite, which is used in making the separator (or bipolar) plates. The availability of composite materials would be useful in achieving these objectives.

8.5 Effective Stack Cooling

Effective stack cooling and utilization of the byproduct heat are required for proper stack operations. Proper ways of achieving these would be developed.

8.6 System Development and Turn-Key Operation

The fuel cell stack needed to be combined in an effective way with a fuel processor and a power-conditioning device. The whole system should be able to operate by pushing a button supplying power demands as needed without any efforts for controlling reactant flows or any adjustments of other parameters. BCS would work towards this goal.

8.7 Mass Production of Fuel Cell Components

For achieving cost reduction, many fuel cell components needed to be mass-produced. BCS was in the process of developing a rapid production method of membrane-electrode assemblies. Separator plates for a stack would be produced from a die with the help a qualified vendor.

8.8 Safety Issues

The work to be undertaken by BCS Fuel Cells, Inc., would involve the use of hydrogen cylinders; and operations of single cells and multi-cell fuel cell stacks. Air would be obtained from the ambient atmosphere using small air compressors. The capacity of an air compressor would vary depending on the size of the fuel cell stack under test. An air compressor would be fitted with a pressure relief valve to release any extra pressure generated in the compressor and not needed for the airflow into the fuel cell. The work would also involve the use of a test bench with flow controls for air and hydrogen and temperature control for the fuel cell stack. Fuel cells would be tested at relatively lower pressures of the reactants, hydrogen and air. Such pressures will be typically 0-3 psig for hydrogen and 0-15 psig for air. Operating temperature would be typically in the range, ambient to 80°C.

The safety plan would be developed and implemented by the Project Manager, Dr. Hari Dhar. He would communicate the plan to the personnel involved in the project, in particular, to personnel involved in any aspect of the work using hydrogen and pressurized air.

BCS had an extensive experience in using hydrogen for fuel cell applications. Such fuel cells have involved the use of single cells of sizes up to 100 cm^2 electrode area, and fuel cell stacks of sizes up to 250 cm^2

area. BCS routinely used hydrogen cylinders fitted with regulators for the source of hydrogen. The experience in the use of hydrogen cylinders and handling of the hydrogen gas in fuel cell tests would be helpful to develop a safety plan and safely perform the tasks for a project.

9. Manufacturing/Engineering Plan

The objectives were to manufacture quality fuel cell stacks at affordable prices. These stacks would be both small and large, convection and standard types. The bipolar plates would be produced in large quantities by molding procedures to achieve cost reduction. At present, graphite is the material for separator plates. Alternative materials, such as metals, would be used when sufficient progress was made in the use of metals as separator plates.

Customer satisfaction and quality control were of top priorities. Each stack would be properly tested, and will be shipped only when found to meet all the criteria for good performances.

As the procedures for assembly of a stack are established, various automations would be introduced in the assembly process.

Dedicated staffs would be required for manufacturing and engineering.

10. Management

Hari Dhar was President of the Company. He cofounded the Company initially receiving a grant from the Center for Space Power, Texas A&M University. He has a Ph.D. degree in Electrochemistry. Hari possesses the skills and vision to work effectively in the emerging fuel cell market. Hari has been working on fuel cells since 1984, first as an Electrochemist with Energy Research Corporation (now Fuel Cell Energy), and then starting BCS in 1989. He has been able to move the Company from the startup to a stage, where the Company can offer products distinguishing itself from others with a new feature. Hari is responsible for management of day-to-day operations, product development, and marketing.

Three advanced machine shops helped supplying company needs in machining.

As the Company operations grow, more personnel for management and various company operations need to be hired. In particular, BCS needs to hire individuals in the capacities of COO, CFO, marketing and sales.

Employees received retirement benefits of 10% of the salary. Key employees would be given special incentives for their jobs. These incentives could be equity distribution, promotion or other financial incentives.

11. Contingencies

Not receiving any grants, low sales would put serious pressure on the company's survival.

12. Financials

The Company sold about 500 stacks of all sizes. The buyers of these stacks were mostly companies and universities around the world buying fuel cells for testing and evaluation purposes.

The unaudited statements of financials of the Company for the initial few years are as follows:

Item	1996	1997	1998	1999
Revenue	134,934	356,413	231,670	205,295
Expenses	135,819	314,943	223,932	204,455
Income before tax	(330)	42,353	12,342	840
Income after tax	(330)	37,668	10,491	714
Total assets	21,872	74,804	75,629	89,484
Total liabilities	4,032	14,232	9,264	22,405
Net worth	17,840	60,572	66,357	67,079

12.1 Sale Projections

Since the Company at this stage was selling mostly smaller stacks for portable applications, the revenue from sales is small ($90,000 in 1999). Once the Company was able to sell power sources for residential and small industrial applications, the revenue would increase dramatically. The revenues for five years following funding are expected to be as follows:

Year 1	Year 2	Year 3	Year 4	Year 5
$750,000	$1,000,000	$2,000,000	$3,000,000	$4,000,000
(40 stacks)	(70 stacks)	(120 stacks)	(200 stacks)	(250 stacks)

The projection was based on sales of about 250 stacks at the end of five years at an average price of $16,000 each. The Company also hopes to generate substantial revenue from sales of its membrane-electrode assemblies for use by other manufacturers. The Company also hoped to generate substantial international sales.

The assumptions for the sales projection were that the Company becomes successful in assembling and testing larger stacks of capacities 5-10kW sizes. The company needed to acquire a larger place for its business, and also needed to hire more personnel for R&D, production, marketing, and management.

The fuel cell market did not grow at a pace near to the initial stage of fuel cell business by various companies. Share values of the companies which went public hovered around the lower price range of the early fluctuations. This is indicative of the overall market situation in the fuel cell business as of this writing (October 2017).

12.3 Market Share

The Company hoped to capture initially 1-2% of the market. As the simplified products of BCS get acceptance by the public, the market share would increase significantly.

13. Financial Needs

About $3 million was sought over a period of two years as investment in the Company.

The Company would need about $1.5 million the first year for R&D on rapid production of various types of MEAs, for more office and laboratory space, hiring more personnel. About $2 million would be needed for the second year tooling for mass production, product development for producing fuel cell systems, continued price reduction efforts, and sales and marketing efforts.

With the increase of Company operations and sales, BCS would be in a position to negotiate successful a merger with or an acquisition by another company. Possible exit strategies for investors were through a merger, acquisition, or an IPO (Initial Public Offering).

Fuel Cell Operation: 3W-5V System (model FCS104)

This fuel cell system was extensively tested for performance and gas leaks within the stack specifications at the company laboratory. It was found to be performing satisfactorily.

The purity of hydrogen could be of industrial grade. The stack is started initially at the room or ambient temperature. It is not necessary to cool the stack to room temperature for subsequent start-up.

The system consists of the following:

- One 4-cell convection fuel cell stack capable of delivering up to 5W at 2.4V when operated alone.
- One control unit (model CBU-4). The control unit consists of the following:
    - One control box
    - One pressure controller
    - One solenoid valve

Care should be taken in making connections of the control unit with the hydrogen source, to the fuel cell stack, and to the electrical load. An electrical load could be an electrical resistance, a small fan, or any small equipment that the customer wants to operate taking power from the fuel cell stack.

The entry of hydrogen is clearly marked in the pressure controller. It will get damaged if hydrogen entry is made in the wrong direction.

In connecting the two electrical wires to the fuel cell stack, make sure that the connection is made right. The positive wire goes to the positive terminal of the stack and the negative wire goes to the negative terminal of the stack. Yellow is +Ve, Black is −Ve.

In connecting the electrical load to the control unit, make sure the positive wire goes to the positive terminal of the load and negative goes to the negative terminal of the load. Red is +Ve, Black is −Ve. If the load is an electrical resistance, then polarity consideration is unimportant.

The control unit can be used in two ways:

- For constant 5V output with power output of max 2.5W. Connect the two wires (INPUT), black to-Ve and yellow to +Ve of the fuel cell stack. Connect the two wires (OUTPUT), black to −Ve and red to +Ve to a load.
- At the learning stage, it may be preferable to operate the fuel cell separately as an independent unit (that is, not using the 5V output box), because the conversion consumes power. Operate the cell for some time, until the temperature reaches 30-50°C. In this temperature range power output from the cell will be more. Then the put heated cell in the conversion circuit. This way, better performance can be obtained.
- Variable voltage output with power output of max 3.5W. Connect the two wires (INPUT) to the fuel cell stack as above. Connect a load across the fuel cell stack. Do not connect the constant voltage output to any load. Make sure these two wires do not touch.

If anytime the stack voltage drops below 2.5V and the control unit lose power, stop operation and restart the stack following the procedures suggested below.

Proceed as follows:

- Put the fuel cell stack and the control box on a clean non-conducting (wood or plastic) table. Keep the table and the surroundings always clean. The stack can be placed little higher on two small pieces

of plastic or wood of thickness 1 cm to 2 cm to facilitate natural convection. Make sure the wood pieces no way block the air convection.
- The pressure controller is set at 10 turns. Turn the knob clockwise all the way. Then make 10 turns counter clockwise. In this position, it will apply about 2 psig on the fuel cell stack. The controller setting tends to change with time. Always check pressure with a pressure gauge in the line.
- Check that the control box is OFF.
- Check that the purge timer knob on the control box is turned all the way to the left. Important: Any time starting the stack, always turn the purge timer knob to the minim um.
- Connect a hydrogen source to the inlet of the pressure controller. It is rated at 150 psig with air. We used inlet pressure of 5-10 psig for hydrogen. The inlet pressure can be possibly 20 psig maximum. It is better to be conservative with the inlet pressure of hydrogen.
- Connect the outlet from the pressure controller to the H_2 In of the stack.
- Connect the leads (black and yellow) from the control box to -- Ve and +Ve terminals of the stack. Use the small screws supplied for making good connections.
- Connect the solenoid valve to the H_2 Out of stack. Make sure that the position of the solenoid valve is always below the hydrogen outlet of the stack. Make sure the exit of the solenoid is horizontal. If the solenoid has moved make the exit horizontal.
- Put a shade on top of the fuel cell stack. The shade helps to facilitate air flow into fuel cell stack. The shade can be made from thicker paper. It is a cylinder of about 5 cm in height and should fit in the top snugly. One shade has been supplied.
- Do not connect a load to the stack yet. We would use the control box itself as the load first and check the operation of the fuel cell system.
- Connect a voltmeter to the fuel cell stack to monitor stack voltage.
- Recheck all connections.
- Turn the switch on the control box ON
- Pass hydrogen to the stack.

- As soon as the main valve for hydrogen has been opened, the ON light should come on and the system should be working. Note that the ON light indicates only that the power is ON. It does not indicate the solenoid ON/OFF time. The solenoid on/off time is indicated by the sound of the solenoid. During the automatic purging, the LED becomes brighter.
- At the minimum position of the purge timer, the interval is 4 sec. Within 30 seconds of the startup, turn the knob to the right to increase the purge interval. The black dot corresponds to about 20 sec interval.

After operation for about 1-3 minutes with the control box as the load, an electrical load can be connected across the 5 V leads for constant voltage output or across the fuel cell stack for variable voltage output. An ammeter can be connected in the line to see the current output from the stack. Also, currents can be calculated if the value of the load resistances is known.

Small 5 V rated equipment, such as a small fan, can be also used as a load.

Cooling fans are not needed for this stack.

The connection of the stack to the hydrogen source should be made with a precision flow control valve. A precision flow control valve is one, which is able to control precisely the hydrogen flow. Without a fine control valve, it may be difficult to pass the required amount of hydrogen to the fuel cell. (Alternatively, one can experiment with whatever control valve one has, and see if that particular valve is able to control the required hydrogen flow).

Occasionally remove accumulated water in the air channels by blowing. Drop in performance is an indication blockage of channels by water accumulation. No elaborate water removal can be placed in a 4-cell stack.

Stopping Operation

- Turn the control box switch OFF
- Stop hydrogen flow
- Turn the purge timer knob to the minimum position

Stack Specifications

Number of cells: 4, Electrode area: 10 cm², Reactants: H_2/air, Mode of H_2 flow: parallel, Mode of airflow: convection, Power output: 3W-5W. Torque on bolts: 20 inch-pound, Max operating temperature: 65°C. For hydrogen operating pressure: 0-3 psig.

Stoichiometry chart for hydrogen flows (ml/min) for 4-cell (3W-5W) convection stack

	Current (A)							
H stoich	0.4	0.6	0.8	1.2	1.5	2.0	2.5	
1.0	11.1	16.7	22.3	27.9	41.8	55.5	69.4	
1.2	13.3	20.0	26.7	33.4	40.1	66.6	83.3	

Operation of 300W Forced-Flow Fuel Cell Stack (model FCS6420)

There are 20 cells in this stack. This is a self-humidified stack. This stack does not require any humidification of reactants. There are four water-cooling cells; black markings on them identify the cells. There is one air-cooling cell. This air-cooling cell is only to be used for measuring temperature inserting a thermocouple at the middle of the stack. Cooling of the stack using fans will not be effective.

This stack has been extensively tested for performance and gas leaks within the stack specifications at the company laboratory. It has been found to be running satisfactorily. We have collected the representative data.

This stack will operate with hydrogen/air, reformate/air. The stack can be also operated with reactants hydrogen/oxygen, but only at the atmospheric pressures of both reactants.

For measurements of cell voltages of individual cells, the entire stack can be divided into groups of four cells. The customer will require meters for measuring voltages of the stack.

The stack has been supplied with a control box unit (model #CBU-4) for regulating the hydrogen flow. The hydrogen pressure controller is on the negative side. The control box and one solenoid (normally open type) have been mounted on the positive side of the stack. The control box has two knobs. Please familiarize with the markings on the control box well. The left hand knob is for controlling the fan speed. The right hand knob is a timer device; it regulates the dead-end time of hydrogen flow from 4-40 seconds. "H_2 out" terminal of the stack needs to be connected to the inlet of the solenoid valve. The control box is powered by fuel cell stack. The stack voltage should not drop below 11.5V. If it does, the control box would be disconnected and the stack would require a startup again.

Precautions

1. For moving or carrying the stack, please hold onto the body of the stack. Do not hold onto any bolts, fittings, and the guiding rods.
2. Protect the guiding rods from breakage. For example, take precautions when moving the stack, when making or removing connection to/from reactant inlets and outlets, or when tightening the bolts.
3. All reactants need to be free from any particles, oil, and grease. Air from a compressor must be filtered.
4. All connections to the stack should be kept free from coming in contact with dust and other particles, oil and grease. For example, when a connection is taken out from the air inlet or outlet of the stack, this end of the tubing should not come in contact with any dust, oil or grease. If it does, then these undesirable particles will find a way inside the stack. Similar care should be taken for the hydrogen inlet and outlet tubing.
5. When the stack is not used for some time, it is recommended that the reactant inlets and outlets are kept closed with some kind of a clean cover. Do not use tapes with grease to close the inlets and outlets. Keep the fuel cell stack needs to be stored in a room having no smell of any chemicals.
6. Avoid using any valves or items using oil or grease. It is recommended that all valves should be opened and the grease cleaned well before using them in the system.
7. Take personal care not to get electrical shocks from the stack. After the running the stack, always bring voltage to zero by drawing power from the stack.
8. When collecting water from the stack, take care that the drainage tube does not touch the water level. This is to avoid back suction of water into the stack. This could be damaging for the cells.

9. When shipping the stack, all inlets and outlets must be closed to prevent dust particles to enter into the stack.
10. Occasionally, torque to each bolt to 25 inch.pound.
11. Familiarize with the operations of the stack at low power outputs first.

Operational Procedures

- Please note that when the stack is operated after a length of time, it is advised to start and operate the stack one to two times before using the stack for a particular application. During this procedure, the performance can pick up.
- Increase the dead-end period for hydrogen flow gradually: 5 sec, 15 sec, 30 sec making sure that at each stage the stack is working properly.
- Higher air pressure and increased dead-end periods will help the self-humidification.
- It is better **not** to operate the stack for longer periods (more than 5-10 minutes) at its limit. So, do not operate long below 12V.

This stack is placed preferably in the following orientation:

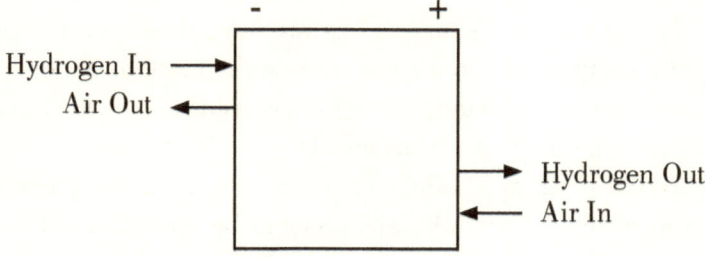

- Place the stack and the control unit on a clean wood or plastic table. Do not allow any tubes to contaminate with dust or other particles.
- Timer knob turned left to the minimum position. The knob regulates the dead-end time, which varies from 4 sec (minimum) to 40 sec (max). The release time is fixed at 0.35 sec. The stack is

usually operated at 15 sec dead-end time. It can also be operated dead-ended, with dead-end time of 30 sec.
- The On/Off switch to Off position.
- Check that the solenoid valve inlet is connected to the "H_2 Out" of the stack.
- Check that the inlet of the solenoid is horizontal for easy removal of water from the hydrogen channels. If the solenoid has rotated, make the inlet horizontal to the table.
- The inlet of solenoid should be at the same level of or lower than the hydrogen outlet of the stack so that water can remove easily from hydrogen channels. Always make sure that water from the hydrogen side can come out freely. Check that the tubes are pointing downward.
- Connect the leads from the control unit to the positive and negative terminals of the stack.
- Connect a hydrogen source to the inlet of the pressure controller. The other end of the pressure controller connects to the "H_2 In" of the fuel cell stack. The inlet pressure of hydrogen to the pressure controller can be about 10 psig or more. The pressure controller is rated at 150 psig with air. With hydrogen, the maximum pressure can be about 10 psig conservatively.
- For monitoring stack temperature, insert a thermocouple into the center of the air-cooling cell. Check that the thermocouple is about the halfway through the hole at the center.
- Stack needs to be cooled with circulation of Distilled water. Water circulation rate of 1-2 liter per minute may be required.
- Start cooling at about 66-67°C and stop cooling at about 65°C. Always make cooling arrangements before starting the stack. Always check that the cooling arrangements are properly made and working. It is better to bypass the stack when testing the cooling arrangement.
- Please note the "Cooling H2O In" and "Cooling H2O Out" ports of the stack. At the opposite side of the stack, the two ports need to be kept blocked for water circulation in the fuel cell stack. We have provided two blocking devices.

- The stack is started initially at the room temperature. For starting subsequently, it is not necessary to bring down the stack to the room temperature.
- Learn operation of the stack initially at lower power outputs.

Stack Startup

Initially purge both sides of the stack to remove accumulated water in the channels.

To purge the air channels, pass air from the top at the rate of 30-40 liter/min for about 10 seconds. Do not purge longer periods. Then do the same with the hydrogen channels also passing air from the top. To purge the H2 side, one needs to disconnect the tubes that connect the pressure controller and the solenoid valve to the stack. Make sure in both cases, the outlets are not blocked. (Keep inlet air pressure within 10 psig). Purging can be avoided when sufficient experience is gained in the stack operation. If the stack is started at about 10A current corresponding to 12-14V at the stack terminal, air purging can be avoided. Purging of the H2 side can be also avoided. However, initially, it is better to follow the purging routines.

We operated the stack without purging either the air or hydrogen side.

For stack operation, air stoichiometry should be around 1.75. Hydrogen can be dead-ended with periodic release. Please note that as the surface conditions of the flow fields change, the reactant stoichiometry can also change.

Air pressure can be 7 psig, and hydrogen pressure can be 3. Stack operation will be facilitated at higher air pressures up to 10 psig. Initial tests can be done for short periods both reactants being at the atmospheric pressures. To apply pressure at the air exit, some kind of a back-pressure device would be required. A thin tubing of ID 1/8" (or thinner) has been supplied with the stack for using at the air side. It will apply 6-7 psig at about 15A. This is a temporary device.

Make electrical connections to the stack. All connecting wires should be as short as possible.

Step by step approach of operating the Fuel Cell stack

When the customer first learns operation of the stack, it is recommended that both air and H2 sides of the stack are purged with air or nitrogen to make sure that there is no water blockage of the channels. Check procedures above.

Connect the "exit tube" supplied at the "Air Out" port. This tube will only apply 6-7 psig at full power and at air stoichiometry of 1.75. Please do not operate more than 3 minutes under these conditions, that is, under low pressures. Pressure of 6-7 psig is only obtained at 15A output; at lower power outputs, the pressure obtained with this exit tube will be much less.

For monitoring stack temperature, insert a thermocouple into the center of the air-cooling cell. Check that the thermocouple is about the halfway through the hole at the center.

The following procedures can be used to check the operation of the fuel cell stack without elaborate arrangement for water-cooling. The stack is operated for a short time and stopped operation before temperature gets above 50°C.

- Check the inlet of solenoid is connected to the "H_2 Out" terminal of the fuel cell stack and that the solenoid inlet is horizontal.
- Check that all other connections of the control unit have been made to the fuel cell stack. This would include two terminals from the control box to the fuel cell stack, volt meter across the stack, current measuring device, connection to electrical load, etc.
- Check that the On/Off switch of the Control Box is OFF, and the timer knob turned to the minimum.
- Pass air at about 6.0 liters per minute (corresponding to air stoichiometry of 1.75 at 10A)
- Pass hydrogen at about 1.6 liters per minute
- Draw power corresponding to about 5A current
- Turn the Control Box switch ON. The LED light should turn on. On/Off sounds of the solenoid should be heard. When the periodic purging occurs, the LED becomes brighter.

- If voltage of all cells and the fuel cell stack are reasonable, increase slowly the power output corresponding to 10A current.
- Operate for 1-2 minutes
- Increase the dead-end period of hydrogen to 15 sec (align the dots)
- At this point the main hydrogen valve can be sufficiently opened to pass enough hydrogen into the stack without further adjustment of the hydrogen flow. The stack will then have the load-following capabilities with respect to hydrogen.
- Increase air flow to about 9 liters per minute (corresponds to air stoich of 1.75 at 15A)
- Draw power output corresponding to 15A current
- Operate for 1-2 minutes
- If everything seems fine, increase the dead-end period to 30 sec.
- Operate 1-2 minutes.

Stop stack operation before stack gets above 50°C.

If the customer has a back pressure device for air flow, try increasing back press above 7 psig, but keeping below 10 psig.

Stopping Operation

- Stop the hydrogen flow. Drain power from the stack and bring down the voltage to a low value. The stop air flow. Disconnect the load.
- When using the control unit, turn Off the switch and let pass hydrogen for 1-2 seconds to that water can come out from the hydrogen channels. Stop hydrogen flow, and proceed as above.
- As the final step, it is also recommended that both sides of the stack be purged again as done before.

Stack Specifications

Number of cells: 20, Electrode area: 64 cm^2, Reactants: H_2/air, reformate/air. Torque on bolts: 25 inch.pound, Power output: 300W. Max operating temperature: 70°C. Operating pressure: 7 psig air, 3-4 psig hydrogen.

Stoichiometry chart for air and hydrogen flow (liters/min) for 20-cell 300W stack

	Current (A)					
Air stoich	5	10	15	20	25	30
1.5	2.6	5.3	8.0	10.4	13.1	15.7
1.75	3.1	6.1	9.1	12.2	15.2	18.3
2.0	3.5	7.0	10.4	13.9	17.4	20.9
H stoich						
1.0	0.694	1.39	2.08	2.78	3.47	4.17
1.1	0.763	1.53	2.29	3.06	3.82	4.59
1.2	0.833	1.67	2.5	3.34	4.17	5.01

Operation of stack at a required power output

After learning stack operation with the above procedures, a required power can be withdrawn from the fuel cell stack. Calculate the amounts of flow rates of air and hydrogen (consult the two tables above) for the required power. Pass the reactants though the stack, and draw that power.

Operation with H_2/O_2

Operate stack at the atmospheric pressures of both reactants. Do not pressurize any reactants. BCS offers a fuel cell specifically for operation with H_2/O_2 that can be operated at higher pressures.

Fuel Cell Operation: 1kW stack (model: 250-24)

Carefully take out the stack from the wooden box it was shipped in. Place the stack on a clean table containing a sturdy piece of plastic in the vertical orientation. Tighten all the 8 bolts to torque 25 inch.pound. Do not loosen, just tighten, or check that they are tight. This is to make sure that the bolts did not get loose during the shipment. The plastic on the table will make sure that no dirt or dust enters the stack when it rests on the table. One or two pieces of plastic are being sent with the stack.

For moving or carrying the stack, please hold onto the body of the stack. Do not hold onto any bolts, fittings, and guiding rods.

Place the stack at the horizontal position such that one can read the lettering in the correct orientation. Please check that the 4 plastic guiding rods are centrally placed with respect to the stack. If the rods have moved, center them by slowly pushing and rotating.

Put the stack back in the vertical orientation until ready to be used or demonstrated. After every use of the stack, remove all tube connections and place the stack in the vertical orientation. When the stack has been cooled to the room temperature, tighten all bolts to 25 inch.pound. Practice this for some time until all the bolts are stabilized.

The customer should contact us immediately if there are any questions on the instruction manual or if there are any problems anytime during operation of the stack.

There are 24 cells in this stack. This is a self-humidified fuel cell stack. This stack does not require any humidification of reactants. This stack has been extensively tested for performance and gas leaks within the stack specifications at the company laboratory. It has been found to be running satisfactorily.

There are four cooling cells placed in the stack. For easy recognition, the cooling cells have been marked with ink dots. From the positive side of the stack: first one is placed after cell #5, second one, after cell #10, third one, after cell #15, fourth one, after cell #20.

Also supplied with this stack is a thermocouple assembly (K-type thermocouple) for connection to the air exit for measurement of inside temperature of the stack. Connect this unit to the Air Out (exit) before starting operation and connect the thermocouple to an appropriate temperature reading meter.

Please read all instructions before operating the stack. It is advised to try the step-by-step procedure for stack operation initially.

Please note the following regarding the fuel cell stack

- Gas inlets and outlets will take tubes of OD (outer diameter) 3/8".
- Water inlets and outlets will take tubes of ID (inside diameter) 3/8". The essential tubes are supplied with the stack.
- Meters, electrical loads, etc. will be required for operation of this fuel cell stack.
- Customer must use a cooling unit for cooling the fuel cell stack during its operation. The coolant liquid can be distilled water.
- It is advised that the operation of this stack be learnt at low power outputs (corresponding to 20A-40A) to familiarize with the working of this fuel cell.
- Peak power output is for a short period only.
- Do not operate the stack below 14V or if any cell drops to 0.5V or lower without correcting the problem.

Precautions:

- For moving or carrying the stack, please hold onto the body of the stack. Do not hold onto any bolts, fittings, and the guiding rods.

- Protect the guiding rods from any breakage. For example, take precautions when moving the stack, when making or removing a connection to/from reactant inlets and outlets, or when tightening the bolts.
- All reactants need to be free from any particles, oil and grease. The air compressor if it gets hot <u>must be</u> cooled from the beginning of the start up.
- All connections to the stack should be kept free from coming in contact with dust and other particles, oil and grease. For example, when a tube is taken out from the air inlet or outlet of the stack, this end of the tubing should not come in contact with any dust, oil or grease. If it does, then these undesirable particles will find a way inside the stack. Similar care should be taken for the hydrogen inlet and outlet tubing. All water connections should be kept clean.
- When the stack is not used for some time, it is recommended that the reactant inlets and outlets, water inlets and outlets are kept closed with some kind of a clean cover to protect the inside from dust and chemicals present in the room. Also, it is a good practice to remove the cooling water from the stack.
- Avoid using any valves or items using oil or grease. It is recommended that all valves should be opened and the grease cleaned very well before using them in the system.
- Take personal care not to get electrical shocks from the stack. During stack operation it is advisable to put on a glove on one hand to avoid an accidental electrical shock. After the running the stack, always bring voltage to zero by drawing power from the stack.
- When collecting water from the stack, take care that the drainage tubes (both air and hydrogen) do not touch the water level. This is to avoid back suction of water into the stack. This could be damaging for the cells.
- After every use of the fuel cell, put the stack at the vertical orientation. When the stack is at the room temperature, torque to each bolt to a pressure of 25 inch.pound.
- Until the torque on bolts has stabilized, after every use please keep the stack in the vertical orientation, that is, one of the metal end

plates resting on the table. After some time when the compression stabilizes, only occasional torqueing will be necessary, and the stack can be kept at the horizontal orientation.
- Check that the bolts are not touching the metal end plates.
- When shipping the fuel cell stack, place it with one of the metal end plates towards base of the container. Place the stack on one or two pieces of sturdy plastic. This way of shipping allows all the weight of the stack to be supported by one of the end plates and protects from breaking of the guiding rods. Always close the gas inlets and outlets, and also the water inlet and outlet holes. Always put enough packing materials so that the stack does not move during shipping. Do not use any packing materials that would crush and become powdery. When shipping, gas inlets and outlets, water inlets and outlets must be closed. Do not use any sticky tapes.

Operation

The following position of the stack is recommended for operation with hydrogen/air.

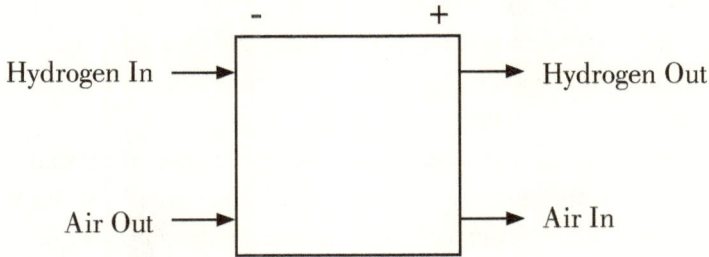

1. Place the stack on a non-conducting table positioning it in a way that one can read the labeling correctly. Keep the table and the surrounding always clean and uncluttered.
2. Make connections to reactant sources. Both reactants must be free of dust, grease, or any particulate matters. Always be careful not to mix up the connections.
3. It is only necessary to tighten the tube connections lightly.

4. Make electrical connections to stack terminals (+ and -) properly. At the same time connect the control unit for hydrogen flow to the stack terminals.
5. Make connections of the two fixtures (one to cooling H2O in, and other to cooling H2O out) and of two flexible tubes to other side of the stack to complete the water flow connection.
6. Make appropriate connections to a heat transfer unit using DISTILLED water as the cooling liquid. Water flow rate of about 2-3 liter per minute would be required. Always check that the circulating water did not pick up any extraneous particles from anywhere in the line. Frequently, change the cooling water with a fresh supply.
7. For measurements of temperature, place a thermocouple at the air outlet. We have provided a thermocouple assembly that fits into the air exit. Please see the attached picture for connection. When the temperature is measured at the exit of airflow, cooling should start at about 66°C and stop at about 63°C.
8. During cooling, the stack performance may drop slightly. But it should recover when the cooling stops.
9. Pass air from the negative side bottom, and hydrogen from the negative side top as marked for reactant entries and exits.
10. The stack is operated initially starting at the room temperature. When starting subsequently, the operation can begin at the temperature of the stack. It is not necessary to cool the stack to the room temperature.
11. At the beginning of stack operation, it is recommended that the stack be flushed with air as follows: flush airside of the stack by passing air at about 40-50 liters/min for about 30 sec. In the same way flush the hydrogen side also. In both cases pass air from the top. Make sure while purging that the outlets are not blocked. It is always safer while purging to keep the inlet pressure of air low (<10 psi).

In the subsequent startup, purge only the air side. It is not necessary to purge the hydrogen side. Only occasional purging can be done if it is suspected that the water buildup in the hydrogen channels is causing some problems. We operated the stack without purging air and hydrogen sides. The above recommendation is for new operators and to make sure that water does not block the channels.

12. The stack is better operated with hydrogen dead-ended with periodic release. The recommended air stoichiometry (stoich) is as follows:

10A	2.0 stoich
20A	1.75 stoich
30A	1.75 stoich
40A	1.75 stoich
50A	1.5 stoich
60A	1.5 stoich
70A	1.5 stoich
80A	1.5 stoich

The air back pressure should be about 7 psig. If hydrogen is not dead-ended, then the recommended stoichiometry of hydrogen is about 1.1 to 1.2 at the hydrogen pressure of about 3-4 psig. Hydrogen can be kept dead-ended with periodic release at back pressure 3-4 psig. Please check the Section on Dead-End Operation for guidelines.

13. The above recommended air stoichs is for a guideline only. As the stack is used for some time, the surface conditions of the flow channels might change. If this happens, the situation may require different stoichiometry. One of the signs that one should look for is the water accumulation or dryness of the channels. For example, does water come out when you purge the channels? Whenever there is an accumulation of water inside the stack, it is a sign that the stack is not getting dry. In that case, stoichiometry can be kept the same or it can be increased little. In the opposite case, the stoich should be decreased.

14. Initially, when starting the stack, stoichiometries of both gases can be slightly higher at stoich 2.0-2.5 air. After performance stabilizes in a minute, decrease stoichiometries to recommended values.

15. Initially, pass enough reactants for 10A current for a few seconds until OCV is fairly stable (20-23V). The inlet hydrogen pressure can be kept at about 5-10 psig, the inlet air pressure can be kept at about 10 psig.
16. Draw power slowly from the stack. Keep air pressure inside the stack about 7 psig and that of hydrogen to low values (within 3-4 psig). A back pressure device is needed to applying pressures to the air and hydrogen sides.

When using a back-pressure device, one should be careful during increasing the flow of air or hydrogen. If the flow is increased at a particular setting of the back-pressure unit, the pressure of the gas can increase suddenly to a high value. To avoid this situation, put the back-pressure unit to a lower setting before increasing the flow, then increase the flow, and again adjust the back-pressure unit if necessary. A good back-pressure control device has the capability of withstanding variation of inlet pressures and gas flows.

17. Adjust reactant flows as needed according to the table provided for this stack.
18. Check the voltage of each quarter. If there is a lower voltage of a particular quarter, determine the cell responsible. The stack may require temporary higher flows of reactants to remove any water blockage of a cell. Alternately, stop operation and purge again.
19. Keep an eye on the rise of temperature as the stack operation proceeds.
20. The final operating temperature is kept within 64°C (measured at the air outlet). Slightly lower limit has been recommended for safety reasons.
21. For stack cooling, circulate distilled water through the stack via a heat exchanger. 2-3 liters per minute of water flow should be sufficient. The temperature guidance is as above in Section 7. When stopping operation, it is not necessary to cool to the room temperature. When the stack is cooled to about 55°C, it can be left to cool on its own by radiation. Remove cooling water from the stack when the stack is not used.

22. Do not operate the stack if the voltage drops below 14V of if any cell drops below 0.5V without correcting the problem.

Stopping Operation

1. To stop operation, stop the hydrogen flow while draining power and bringing down the voltage to a low value. Then stop the airflow. Immediately release air and hydrogen pressures inside the stack.
2. After the stack operation has been stopped, flush airside of the stack by passing air at about 40-50 liters/min for about 30 seconds. Make sure while purging that the outlets are not blocked. It is always safer while purging to keep the inlet pressure of air low (<10 psi).

It is also recommended that when starting the stack, the above flushing procedure be repeated. This will remove any water blockage that might have accumulated during the period the stack was cooling.

3. Put the stack in the vertical orientation until the torque on bolts has stabilized. This practice would avoid strain on the plates and the guiding rods in the event that bolts become loose.

Storing

When the stack is not used for anytime, please close all inlets and outlets. Do not use sticky tapes. It is better to store in the vertical orientation.

Step by Step Approach of operating the stack

The stack should not be operated more than five minutes under these conditions at the atmospheric pressures.

This procedure can be used to check if the stack is working or not.

Initially, the customer may want to see right away the operation of the stack. Follow the procedures given below:

- Flush the stack as detailed above.
- Make proper electrical connections, air, and hydrogen connections to the stack.
- Place the thermocouple assembly at the air exit. Connect the thermocouple to a reading meter.
- Pass air at about 8.5 liters per minute (flow corresponds to 2 stoichiometry at 10A)
- Pass hydrogen at about 2.0-2.5 liters per minute.
- Note the OCV. This should be about 20-23V.
- Draw about 10A of current
- Operate for a few minutes (1-3 minutes)
- Increase air flow to about 15 liter/min (stoich about 1.75 at 20A) and hydrogen flow to about 4.0 liter/min.
- Draw power corresponding to about 20A of current. Operate for 1-3 minutes.
- Increase air flow to about 22 liter/min (stoich about 1.75 at 30A) and hydrogen flow to about 6 liter/min.
- Draw power corresponding to about 30A of current. Operate for 1-3 minutes.
- Increase air to about 30 liters per minute (stoich about 1.75 at 40A current).
- Operate for about 1-3 minutes.
- Note the temperature. When the temperature approaches 45-50°C, stop stack operation.

When back pressure devices are available, the above procedures can be repeated at air pressure of about 7 psig and hydrogen pressure of about 3-4 psig.

How to Decrease Power Output

Operation of the stack can be stopped anytime by stopping the H2 flow and following the procedures outlined below under heading "Stopping Operation".

To increase the output, follow the above procedures outlined under heading "Step by Step Approach". Basically, increase air flow and then increase power output. To decrease the power output, first adjust the electrical load to the low value and then adjust the air flow quickly. The process of lowering the output can be done in steps: for example, 40A to 30A to 20A, etc.

Operation with Reformate

The stack will also operate with reformate/air. Please find by experiments the suitable stoichiometry of reformate for stack operation. When using reformate (dilute fuel) as the fuel, the purge timer for hydrogen flow cannot be used.

Stack Operation under dead-ending hydrogen with periodic release

This stack should be preferably operated under dead-ending hydrogen with periodic release. Operation under such conditions conserves water inside the stack and helps the self-humidification process. The customer needs a control unit to regulate the hydrogen flow. The dead-end period can be initially 15 sec and can be increased to 30 sec depending on the experience with the stack (that is how well the stack performs). We used dead-end period up to 30 sec while testing the stack.

Stoichiometry Chart for air and hydrogen flows (liters/min) for 24-cell stack

Air stoich		Current (A)								
		10	20	30	40	50	60	70	80	90
1.5		6.3	12.5	18.8	25.1	31.3	37.6	43.8	50.1	56.4
1.75		7.3	14.6	21.9	29.2	36.5	43.8	51.2	58.5	65.8

2.0		8.4	16.7	25.1	33.4	41.8	50.1	58.5	66.8	75.2	
Hydrogen stoich											
1.0		1.7	3.3	5.0	6.7	8.4	10.0	11.7	13.4	15.0	
1.1		1.87	3.6	5.5	7.4	9.2	11.0	12.87	14.74	16.5	
1.2		2.0	4.0	6.0	8.0	10.0	12.0	14.0	16.0	18.0	

Health Issues

My life, my work, and my business venture, everything seems to be going smoothly. The routine of constant work in my business kept me busy and fruitful. My daily meditation routine kept me fit and stress-free. I slept deep and woke up fresh. Always ready to go to office in the morning reaching there usually by 7:45AM. Whenever life goes smoothly always be prepared for the unexpected. Suddenly, I found myself in the midst of problems in my business office that affected my health. Within a short period of time by blood pressure increased such that I had to start a medication for reducing my blood pressure. I had to undergo cardiac stress tests, have CT of my brain and MRI scans of my brain and blood vessels, several blood tests all to diagnose the reason of my physical discomfort. Immediately, no good reason was diagnosed so that a suitable medication could be prescribed for alleviating the actual problem.

Among possible reasons for discomfort with health problems, there was a switch box on my computer table, connections leading to two computers providing Internet connections and a printer. The switch box may have generated undesirable radiation effects continuous exposures to which became reasons for physical discomforts. It is like a laptop computer should not be kept in the lap most of the time.

I have been meditating following the Kriya yoga techniques in the tradition of Baba Hariharananda of the Kriya Yoga Institute since February 1999. This is about eight years span up to December 2007. Prior to this I followed the Kriya yoga techniques as taught by Roy Eugene Davis of the Center for Spiritual Awareness for about two years. Prior to this I was practicing basic techniques of meditation since about 1991. So, it is about more than 15 years I have been a practitioner of meditation. I have derived immense benefits from regular meditation.

In the month of August or early September 2007, one day in the evening during my usual Kriya meditation time starting at about 5:30 PM, I felt a slight pressure on my heart. The meditation technique involves some yogic exercise postures that require a certain degree of strenuous physical fitness for successful completion of the Kriya meditation routine. I kind of eased the meditation routine that day and the subsequent days to prevent the recurrence of the chest tightness. After a few days, I felt better, and watched myself about two weeks. I had a feeling of chest tightness again a few times unusually at end of work day with the feeling of general body weakness. Middle of October was the time I had to attend the Fuel Cell Seminar at San Antonio. I decided that before I attend the conference I should have a check up on my heart. I called my doctor's office. My primary care physician checked me and found me all right, but advised that I should consult a cardiologist at the Scott and White health center, my health insurance carrier. The heart specialist may suggest further tests if needed. This I could do after I came back from the conference. The doctor advised me to start taking a daily low dosage of aspirin, which has been known to aid condition of the blood flow and the heart.

New Business Location and Business Closure

The problems of entry of cigarette smokes from an adjacent unit into our unit at the Finfeather Road facility became a constant nuisance for some time. We had to find a new location. We purchased one acre land in a business district at the Bryan city limit and got made a facility of about 2000 square feet, which is about double the size of the old location. In the latter part of 2009, we moved to the new location at 8036 Wickson Ridge Drive in Bryan.

Early 2010 when I was going for a walk in the afternoon I felt short of breath. I was not sure if that was a limitation for continuing walking. Gradually, the short of breath became worse and I was not able to continue walking. I used to carry a cell phone. One day in the walking routine I had to call my wife to pick me up. Next day, I made an appointment with Dr. McIlhaney, my primary care physician. He understood the problem, made an EKG of my heart. The EKG was normal. He, however, told me that he would talk to my cardiologist, Dr. Glamann, who called me and setup an urgent appointment for more tests for any heart blockage. More tests revealed that I had blockages in two arteries, which needed to be removed urgently through surgery. He recommended a heart surgeon for performing the operation.

On April 8, 2010 I underwent double bypass heart surgery. I came out of the surgery all right, and started walking in the hospital. I was informed of a facility connected to the hospital where there is a program of exercise for heart patients. I exercised for one hour with exercise machines three days a week. Initially, I felt all right. Gradually, it seemed that one hour exercise was too much. My blood pressure increased and I felt tired whole day. The medicines I was taking and the side effects I could not tolerate. The recovery supposed to take three to six months. I did not recover well. The large keloids on the scar of the operation were very bothersome. That means the surgery did not go well for me. For few years I tried to get rid of the keloids going to a plastic surgeon. He injected steroids into the keloids. It helped initially to some extent, but the keloids came back after sometime. I underwent another surgery by the plastic surgeon to remove the keloids. Keloids seem to grow and become source of almost constant pain. In our daughter's marriage ceremony at the end of December 2010, I could not attend the wedding reception and give my welcoming speech.

Towards the end of 2011, my health became worse. It was not possible to continue further with my company. The business closed officially on December 31, 2011. I did not get any offer from anyone to get rights of our intellectual property. I found a customer for the land and business facility. I was also able to sell the instrumentation used to do the company business. I received a good lump sum. Looking back, I find it was worthwhile to get a new facility, owning it outright, for the company business. I could accumulate the amounts I would have spent for the rental for about two and a half years. I operated the business for 22 years. I was 68 years old when the business had to be closed. I desired another 5-10 years of continuation the business. But that did not happen.

Also, that I was unable to form a partnership with a suitable person having similar interests as mine. I was not able to proceed further beyond what I achieved. I am deeply inundated to my elder brother for his sacrifices which facilitated my education and training. I thank my wife, the family and extended family members for their moral supports. I thank God for bestowing me with this life and letting me go through the experiences I endured.

Biography of Haripada Dhar

Dr. Dhar received (1973) his Ph.D. degree in Chemistry specializing in Electrochemistry from the University of Ottawa, Canada, under the guidance of Dr. Brian E. Conway, a prominent electrochemist. His Ph.D. thesis work dealt with investigations on the studies of electrical double layer. Earlier, he received his Master's degree from Saint Francis Xavier University, Antigonish, Nova Scotia, Canada.

Dr. Dhar is the President of BCS Fuel Cells, Inc. He has established himself as a leader in the PEM (proton exchange membrane) fuel cell industry offering simplified and easy-to-operate fuel cells and systems. Dr. Dhar is an electrochemist having both academic and industrial experiences. He has a strong background in work related to fuel cell development. He has carried out half-cell measurements related to hydrogen oxidation and oxygen reduction on gas diffusion electrodes. He carried out detailed investigations on the extent of catalyst poisoning by CO (carbon monoxide) present in hydrogen fuels. He has carried out optimization studies on the development of high power density fuel cells, and regenerative fuel cells. He is one of the early leaders in the development of self-humidified fuel cells, including designing and building PEM fuel cell stacks and systems. The work in the PEM fuel cell area has led to the issuance of 4 US patents. Dr. Dhar has introduced about 15 models of stacks and systems for sale and has sold about 500 fuel cell stacks and systems. He has about 45 publications, including 5 patents and 2 book articles. He has authored one book, "Something Worth Reading for Inspiration", published in June 2017.

He received unsolicited letters of appreciations from customers around the world using his fuel cell products: membrane-electrodes assemblies and fuel cell stacks of various capacities. He received an unsolicited letter of congratulations (appreciations) from the eminent electrochemist Dr. John O'M. Bockris, who was his supervisor and mentor at Texas A&M University. Dr. Bockris was an advocate of for the use of clean fuel, hydrogen, related to fuel cell operations.

He is an initiate in the *Kriya Yoga* meditation in the lineage of *Babaji*, learning the technique from yoga masters, Roy Eugene Davis of the Center for Spiritual Awareness and from *Paramahamsa Hariharananda* of the *Kriya Yoga* Institute. He attended several *Kriya Yoga* retreats.

Publication List of H. P. Dhar

1. Molecular orientation in adsorption of pyridine and pyrazine at water/mercury and water/air interfaces. B. E. Conway, H. P. Dhar, and S. Gottesfeld. *J. Colloid and Interface Science.* **43**(1975)303.
2. On adsorption isotherms for substitutional adsorption of molecules of different sizes. H. P. Dhar, B. E. Conway, and K. M. Joshi. *Electrochimica Acta.* **18**(1973)789.
3. Solvent structure and molecular orientation in the double layer at the mercury/water interface. B. E. Conway and H. P. Dhar. *Croatia Chemica Acta.* **45**(1973)109.
4. Solvent structure and molecular orientation behavior of adsorbed pyridine and pyrazine at the mercury/water interface. B. E. Conway, J. Mathieson, and H. P. Dhar. *J. Phys. Chem.* **78**(1974)1226.
5. Compensation effects in the thermodynamics of electrochemical adsorption of organic substances. B. E. Conway and H. P. Dhar. *Colloid and Polymer Science.* **253**(1975)11.
6. Hydration co-sphere and ion-pair interactions in electrochemical adsorption of organic N-cations. B. E. Conway and H. P. Dhar. *J. Colloid and Interface Science.* **48**(1974)73.
7. Adsorption behavior of 1,4-diazabicyclo octane at the mercury electrode. B. E. Conway and H. P. Dhar. *Electrochimica Acta.* **19**(1974)445.
8. On selection of standard states in adsorption isotherms. B. E. Conway and H. P. Dhar. *Electrochimica Acta.* **19**(1974)5.

9. Preliminary communication on molecular size factor and evaluation of interaction in terms in electrochemical isotherms. B. E. Conway and H. P. Dhar. *Surface Science.* **44**(1974)261.
10. On adsorption pseudo capacity. B. E. Conway and H. P. Dhar. *Discussion of Faraday Society.* **56**(1973).
11. Comparison of surface tension and electrochemical adsorption measurements from capillary electrometer and mercury drop-time techniques. F. Kimmerle, H. Mennard, B. E. Conway, and H. P. Dhar. *Electrochimica Acta.* **19**(1974)883.
12. Gas-solid exchange reactions: Zinc vapor and polycrystalline zinc orthosilicate. E. A. Secco, H. P. Dhar, and Chien-Hou Su. *Can. J. Chemistry.* **42**(1974)3932.
13. Study of combined electroreflectance and double-layer effects on lead electrodes. H. P. Dhar. *Surface Science.* **66**(1977)449.
14. An electrochemical system for production of hydrogen and heavy water from off-peak electricity. S. Das Gupta, H. P. Dhar, J. Jacobs, and S. Mohanta. *Proc. Symp. on Industrial Water Electrolysis,* Vol 78-4, p. 282. Electrochemical Society Incorporated, Pennington, New Jersey.
15. Electrochemical inactivation of marine bacteria. H. P. Dhar, J. O'M. Bockris and D. H. Lewis. *J. Electrochem. Soc.* **128**(1981)229-231.
16. New trends in electrolytic reactor materials: Diaphragms. M. Islam, N. P. White, H. P. Dhar, and S. Das Gupta. *Polymer Plastic Technology Engineering.* **15**(1980)61-82.
17. Electrochemical diminution of surface bacterial concentration. H. P. Dhar, D. H. Lewis, and J. O'M. Bockris. *Can. J. Microbiol.* **27**(1981)998-1010.
18. A cathodic electrochemical method for microbial fouling prevention. H. P. Dhar, J. O'M. Bockris, and D. H. Lewis. *U.S. Patent No. 4,440,611.* 1984.
19. Use of in-situ electrochemical reduction of oxygen in diminution of adsorbed bacteria on metals in seawater. H. P. Dhar, D. W. Howell, and J. O'M. Bockris. *J. Electrochem. Soc.* **129**(1982)2178-2182.
20. Electrodeposition of cobalt tetraazaannulene dibromide on graphite electrodes. M. Yamana, R. Darby, H. P. Dhar, and R. E. White. *J. Electroanal. Chem.* **152**(1983)261-268.

21. The effect of heat treatment atmospheres on the electrocatalytic activity of cobalt tetraazaannulenes. H. P. Dhar, R. Darby, V. Y. Young, and R. E. White. *Electrochimica Acta.* **30**(1985)423-429.
22. Corrosion behavior of 70:30 Cu:Ni alloy in 0.5 M NaCl and in synthetic seawater. H. P. Dhar, R. E. White, R. Darby, R. B. Griffin, and G. Burnell. *Corrosion.* **41**(1985)193-196.
23. Corrosion of Cu and Cu:Ni alloys in 0.5 M NaCl and in synthetic seawater. H. P. Dhar, R. E. White, R. Darby, R. B. Griffin, G. Burnell, and L. R. Cornwell. *Corrosion.* **41**(1985)317-323.
24. Electrochemical methods for prevention of microbial fouling. H. P. Dhar. *Modern Biochemistry.* Eds. H. Keyzer and F. Gutman. Plenum Press, New York, 1986. Chapter 22, pp. 593-606.
25. Performance study of a fuel cell Pt-on-Carbon anode in presence of CO and CO_2, and calculation of adsorption parameters of CO poisoning. H. P. Dhar, L. G. Christner, A. K. Kush, and H. C. Maru. *J. Electrochemical Society.* **133**(1986)1574.
26. On the effect of the Fe^{2+}/Fe^{3+} redox couple on oxidation of carbon in hot phosphoric acid. H. P. Dhar, L. G. Christner, and A. K. Kush. *J. Electroanal. Chem.* **213**(1986)161-167.
27. Modeling of CO poisoning of a fuel cell anode. H. P. Dhar, A. K. Kush, D. N. Patel, and L. G. Christner. *Electrochemical and Thermal Modeling of Batteries and Fuel Cells.* Eds. J. R. Selman and H. C. Maru. The ECS Softbound Proceeding Series, Princeton, N. J. 1986. pp. 284-297.
28. Nature of CO adsorption during hydrogen oxidation in relation to modeling for CO poisoning of a fuel cell anode. H. P. Dhar, L. G. Christner, and A. K. Kush. *J. Electrochem. Soc.* **134**(1987)3021-3026.
29. Corrosion of graphite composites in phosphoric acid fuel cells. L. G. Christner, H. P. Dhar, M. Farooque, and A. K. Kush. *Corrosion.* **43**(1987)571-575.
30. A new concept for high-cycle-life LEO: Rechargeable MnO_2-Hydrogen. A. J. Appleby, H. P. Dhar, Y. J. Kim, and O. J. Murphy. *J. Power Sources.* **29**(1990)333-340.

31. Utilization of dissolved oxygen in water in preventing microbial fouling on metals. H. P. Dhar. *Electrochemistry in Transition: 20th to 21st Century.* Plenum Press, New York, 1991.
32. On the effect of magnetic field on electrophoresis. H. P. Dhar, S. Nath, and D. H. Lewis. *Texas J. Science.* **43**(1991)334-336.
33. A unitized approach to solid polymer electrolyte fuel cell. H. P. Dhar. *J. Applied Electrochem.* **23**(1993)32-37.
34. On solid polymer fuel cells. H. P. Dhar. *J. Electroanal. Chemistry.* **357**(1993)237-250.
35. Near ambient, unhumidified solid polymer fuel cell. H. P. Dhar. *U.S. Patent No. 5,242,764* (1993).
36. Near ambient unhumidified solid polymer fuel cell. H. P. Dhar. *U.S. Patent No. 5,318,863.* 1994.
37. Recent progress in proton exchange membrane fuel cells. N. K. Anand, A. J. Appleby, and H. P. Dhar, et al. *Proceedings of the 10th Hydrogen Energy Conference.* Cocoa Beach, FL. June 20-24, 1994. Vol 3. 1669-1679.
38. Internally humidified proton exchange membrane fuel cell. *Proceedings of the 29th Intersociety Energy Conversion Engineering Conference.* Vol. 2, pp. 865-870. 1994.
39. Method for catalyzing a gas diffusion electrode. H. P. Dhar. *U.S. Patent No. 5,521,020. 1996.*
40. Internally humidified high performance proton exchange membrane fuel cell. *1994 Fuel Cell Seminar.* Pub. Courtesy Associates, Inc. Washington, D.C. pp. 85-88.
41. Flow facilitator for improving operation of a fuel cell. H. P. Dhar, K. A. Lewinski. U.S. Patent #5,935,725 (1999).
42. Simplified proton exchange membrane fuel cells for space and terrestrial applications. H. P. Dhar, K. A. Lewinski, and V. K. Tripathi. Proceedings of the Space Technology & Applications International Forum (STAIF). January 1998. Albuquerque, NM.
43. Medium-term stability testing of proton exchange membrane fuel cell stacks as independent power units. H. P. Dhar. *J. Power Sources,* 143(2005)185-190.

44. Measurements of fuel cell internal resistances for the detection of electrode flooding. H. P. Dhar and S. K. Chaudhuri. *J. Solid State Electrochemistry.* 13(7)(2009)999.
45. Detection and verification of electrode flooding in single cell studies. H. P. Dhar and S. K. Chaudhuri. *ECS Transactions,* Vol. 17 (2009).

References

1. Fuel Cell Handbook. A. John Appleby and F. R. Foulkes. Publisher: Van Nostrand Reinhold. 1989.
2. Modern Electrochemistry. J. O'M. Bockris and A. K. N. Reddy. Publisher: Springer Science and Business Media. 2007.
3. PEM Fuel Cells: Theory and Practice. Frano Barbir. Publisher: Elsevier Science. 2005.
4. Fuel Cells Fundamentals. Ryan O'Hayre, Suk-Won Cha, Whitney Colella, and F. B. Prinz. Publisher: Wiley. 2009.
5. Build your Own Fuel Cells. Philip Hurley. Publisher: Good Idea Creative Services. 2013.
6. Hydrogen and Fuel Cells. B. Sorensen. Publisher: Academic Press. 2011.
7. Fuel Cells: Principles, Design and Analysis. S. T. Revankar and P. Majumdar. Publisher: CRC Press. 2016.
8. Starting a High-Tech Business Venture. Eric Koester. Publisher: CRC Press. 2009.
9. Managing Dynamic Technology-Oriented Businesses. Dariusz Jemielniak. Publisher: IGI Global. 2012.
10. Successful Marketing Strategy for High-Tech Firms. Eric Viardot. Publisher: Artech House. 2004.
11. Something Worth Reading for Inspiration. Haripada Dhar. Publisher: Xlibris. 2017.

www.ingramcontent.com/pod-product-compliance
Lightning Source LLC
Chambersburg PA
CBHW020450220526
45464CB00002B/931